N D

O

:64

MODERN PAINTING

THIS VOLUME, EDITED
BY ANDRÉ GLOECKNER,
WAS FIRST PUBLISHED
IN NINETEEN HUNDRED
AND FIFTY-ONE BY THE
HYPÉRION PRESS, PARIS.
PRINTING OF THE TEXT,
ENGRAVINGS AND COLOR-
PLATES BY IMPRIMERIE
CRÉTÉ, CORBEIL, FRANCE.

HISTORY OF

MODERN PAINTING

Published under the supervision of

GERMAIN BAZIN

Curator of the Museum of the Louvre,
Professor at the École du Louvre.

Translated from the French by
ROSAMUND FROST

Text, research, illustrations, biographies, bibliography by
GASTON DIEHL, MARC LOGÉ, MADELEINE LECLERC,
M. DE GESNE, FREDERICK MOSS, S. BÉGUIN

Published by
THE HYPERION PRESS, NEW YORK - PARIS - LONDON
Distributed by
THE MACMILLAN COMPANY NEW YORK

CONTENTS

ART IN THE 19th CENTURY

FRANCE

IT may be said that no period in art is as varied and complex and, at the same time, as rich in popular appeal as that which extends from the year 1785 when David exhibited *The Oath of the Horatii* to 1926 when Claude Monet, the father of Impressionism, closed his eyes on his terrestrial lily-pools. It was an era of profound and radical changes whose revolutionary surge swelled on the ocean of philosophical and political thought at a time when the idea paramount in men's minds was liberty.

The French Revolution fired the imagination of Jacques-Louis David whose fame, at the age of 49, was already well established. David was the first to realize that contemporaneous events may be a fitting subject for a great painting. His various functions in the government of the new Republic were admirably suited to his passionate temperament and gave him a first-hand knowledge of the events he so strikingly depicted. His style is epic but he achieves grace. The immense canvases painted during his Napoleonic period to the glory of the Emperor show as keen a sense of form and composition as his delicate portraits of *Madame Sériziat* or of the youthful *Madame Récamier*.

David's search for beauty of form, style and decorative arrangement excluded color and movement. Most of his followers stiffened under his tyrannic rule. Gérard and Guérin, the master of Géricault and Delacroix, carried the pseudo-classical style to the highest degree of severity. Some reacted against it, and the pathetic loyalty of Gros who, torn between the lure of Romanticism and the stern demands of David's classicism thought himself a failure and committed suicide, shows the power of the master's influence on the men of his day.

The greatest of David's direct pupils, Ingres, was primarily a draughtsman for whom the musical effect of line, the purity of contour and the grace of arabesque were an innate necessity; he was almost as gifted a musician as he was a painter. His favorite saying was, "Drawing is the integrity of art." He held with David that color was subordinated to line and composition, but he differed from his master in his general conception of art, going back still farther into the past, as far as Raphael, choosing classical themes instead of modern subjects.

The teaching of Ingres and his mastery, particularly in depicting the nude,

DAVID.—The Oath of the Horatii.   Paris, Musée du Louvre.

Painted at Rome in 1784, this picture, which attempts to recreate antiquity as accurately as possible, is composed of independent groups silhouetted like a bas-relief against the background.   The cold tones contribute toward a sculptural appearance.

had far-reaching effects. Since his day there has been an everlasting struggle between "official" or "academic" art and spontaneous expression. The academic painters continued in the vein of Ingres, but few attained his cold perfection.   Most of them, although famous in their day, have become examples of artificiality, melodrama and bad taste; we need only mention Bouguereau and Cabanel. Couture, Delacroix, Gérôme and Gleyre, a Swiss, are chiefly remembered as teachers who trained another generation of academic painters.   Meissonnier and Detaille, in their army pictures, carried precision to a fault, every detail given the same importance, the result a piece of elaborate craftsmanship of documentary interest only.

DAVID.—Madame Sériziat.   Paris, Musée du Louvre.

This graceful portrait of his sister-in-law, painted in 1795, shows that,
if David often strives toward the exaltation of virility, he has retained from
18th century a feeling of feminine grace.

Gros.—The Battle of Eylau.   Paris, Musée du Louvre.

Having been formed by a classical discipline, Gros still composes his picture with juxtaposed figures that develop into a frieze against the background: but, with a new kind of boldness, he paints close-ups of the dead bodies and he places the action in an admirable winter landscape.

A review of the Romantic movement cannot be restricted to the domain of pictorial art. In literature, in music as well as in painting, it seeped through almost simultaneously in several countries and swelled into an overwhelming current. Whenever the artist's personality predominates, whenever art is an outlet for subjective feeling and lyrical emotion, the spirit of Romanticism prevails. The movement became conscious of itself in 1827. Victor Hugo's manifesto, in his "Preface to Cromwell," published in 1827, defined its aims and doctrines. It was freedom at last for the artist to vibrate with whatever moved him.

There were forerunners, such as Prud'hon and Gros. But the first real manifestation of the Romantic spirit was Géricault's *Raft of the Medusa*, exhibited in 1819. The huge canvas shows the survivors of the French frigate which had foundered on its way to Senegal in 1816. The outcry against this powerful work was immediate and unanimous. Its subject, its emotional treatment, its size, all were condemned. Géricault had prepared his masterpiece as thoroughly as Leonardo or Holbein; he had observed stormy seas and the movements of a miniature raft made to scale, had spent days in a hospital studying the features of the sick and dying and made drawings of corpses in various positions. He was understood by one man only, his friend and fellow-student Delacroix who posed for the dying man on the extreme left.

Delacroix was to draw the attention of art critics three years later when he exhibited *Dante and Virgil Ferried Across the Styx*, painted in a similar vein. A passionate colorist and a master of movement, he was influenced by Gros and also, in 1824, by Constable whose manner of painting in "broken color" bore the seeds of Impressionism.

The Massacres of Scio, which he repainted after having seen Constable's *Haywain*, placed him at the head of the Romantic school. From the first, his manner, in which light and shadow are paramount while draughtsmanship is sometimes sacrificed to expression, was the exact opposite of the Neo-Classic style of Ingres.

As David had been served by the Napoleonic epoch, so was Delacroix borne on the crest of the Revolution of 1830. He found expression for patriotism in an exalting canvas, *Liberty at the Barricades*, a painting as far from the heroic but frozen scenes of David as his glowing and sometimes sinister colors are far from the pseudo-classic painter's subdued and grayish tints.

The battle between Ingres and Delacroix, the cool, composed draughtsman and the fiery colorist, passionately divided public opinion at the same time as the battle between the Classics and Romantics in literature. The first half of the 19th century saw the triumph of youth and enthusiasm over the stiff concepts of an earlier generation.

Gros.—Bonaparte at Arcola.   Paris, Musée du Louvre.

Gros, who had followed the army to Italy, painted Bonaparte in the heat of action, spurring on his hesitating soldiers to the attack of the bridge of Arcola.

DAVID.—The Coronation of Napoleon (detail). Paris. Musée du Louvre.

A magnificent grouping of portraits, The Coronation is still composed in David's "statuesque" manner, with figures either full-face or in profile; but the artist's palette derives rich effects from the sumptuous costumes.

.D.—Madame Récamier.   Museum of Fine Arts of the City of Paris.

ard has portrayed the beautiful and mysterious Madame Récamier in the
.tyle of antiquity; but there is already something Romantic about the languor
of her pose.

GÉRICAULT.—The Madwoman.   Museum of Lyons.

Géricault's instinct for realism incited him to study the effects of the decomposi-
tion of the body and to analyse psychological defects.   At the end of his life,
he made an entire series of portraits in a mental institution.

Delacroix had no direct pupils, but the exoticism of his art and his penetrating articles in the "Revue des Deux-Mondes" formed a school of Romantic painters true to his creed. Following the behest of the master, many painters went for inspiration to Morocco and Algiers or to the Orient, a thing unheard of in the Neo-Classic days. Of such were Fromentin, a distinguished writer, Decamps, Marilhot.

Ingres and Delacroix both excelled in mural painting and revived this branch of art which had fallen into 18th century prettiness. The cold color and precise design of Ingres was particularly suited to decoration. The Romantic painter's vehement eloquence lacked the simplicity and restfulness desirable in wall painting, but the beauty of his rich, well-balanced compositions compensates by far the lost serenity of the Neo-Classic.

Chassériau, an extremely gifted pupil of Ingres from the age of 10, was a Romantic in the true sense of the word. He died in the prime of life and his best work, the decoration of the Cour des Comptes, was unfortunately destroyed during the Commune. Some fragments of it remain; from these and from his canvases we know that he allied purity of line to warmth of color.

Puvis de Chavannes, a contemporary of the Impressionists, followed the impulse given by Chassériau, devoting his life to mural decoration, which he considered the chief object of painting. He was as inspired a dreamer in his immense compositions as the English painter Blake in his minute watercolors. Before starting to work, he waited for a "vision" to descend upon him and when his painting was complete in his mind's eye he would carry it out first on a small scale, in his peculiar stylized manner, and then, using black and white only, in its true size.

With the development of Romanticism, landscape painting, hitherto of secondary importance, came to the fore. In the days of Nicolas Poussin and Claude le Lorrain, landscape was appreciated chiefly as a setting for bucolic scenes and seldom for its own sake. Hills, crags, woodland dells and pastures bore no sign of local color. But with the new comprehension of nature, as developed by pre-Romantic writers, such as J.-J. Rousseau, a tendency appeared to regard landscape as a subject worthy of representation in itself. The painter who emancipated it from its dependency and made it a free expression, while keeping it in the serene path of classicism, was Camille Corot.

Corot is the poet of dawn, of silence on sleeping waters, of pensiveness and calm. The Italian inspiration of his early works does not preclude a manner wholly personal in the treatment of light and shadow. Corot was enamored of nature and often painted out of doors at sunrise; his late art is a further step toward Impressionism. But he is the poet of fleeting emotion whereas the Impressionists were inspired by fleeting vision alone.

GÉRICAULT.—The Raft of the Medusa (detail).   Paris, Musée du Louvre.
To paint a contemporary event in the colossal dimensions which had been reserved until then solely for historical painting was an example of Romantic daring.   The diagonal composition is equally Romantic, but the heroic physiques of the castaways are still in the tradition of David.

The rendering of this emotion is greatly enhanced by Corot's exquisite sense of values.   He was so conscious of their importance that he invented a system of notation for them, graduating them in a scale of intensity ranging from 1 to 7.

While Corot, about 1830, resorted to the glades of Fontainebleau to seek there the settings of his Neo-Classic landscapes, the Romantics, in the wake of Theodore Rousseau, penetrated into the depths of the forest, in search of the mystery of universal life.   Their group was called the Barbizon

GEORGES MICHEL.—The Mill.   London, Victoria and Albert Museum, Ionides Collection.—*Finding his inspiration in the Dutch masters, Georges Michel was, as early as the end of the 18th century, the first to paint the grandeur of hazy skies covering immense plains; he sought his motifs on Montmartre which was then a rural hill dotted with windmills.*

DUPRÉ.—A Squall. Private Collection.

Jules Dupré, like Théodore Rousseau, was captivated by the depths of the forest of Fontainebleau; but, unlike the master of Barbizon, he was also attracted by the sea which he often painted along the coast of the Channel, either in France or England.

School from the name of the village where they found shelter. In their quest for virgin nature, they followed the examples of 17th century Dutch landscape painters, especially Ruysdael and Hobbema, and also of English artists, such as Crome and Constable.

Théodore Rousseau was tormented all his life by the desire to attain, by means of patient observation based on minute analysis, the secret of organic life, of trees, earth and sky. Jules Dupré, who was also a marine painter and who led the way for the Impressionists by his rendition of Normandy skies, followed Théodore Rousseau into the forest of Fontainebleau. Diaz de la Peña, a pupil of Rousseau, also depicted its shady and rocky solitude. The sun-flecked landscapes of Daubigny, the poet of water, are more akin to the evanescent emotion of Corot. One of his works was to give a decisive impulse to Claude Monet.

Romanticism gave rise about 1848 to another movement called Realism. Opposed to the imagination that made the painters of 1830 turn to history, legend or exoticism, it aimed at expressing the life of contemporary people. Millet, Courbet, Daumier in various ways illustrated this tendency.

Millet went to live at Barbizon in 1848 and studied on the outskirts of the forest the work of the peasants. The emotion of Corot, his love of nature, his exquisite poetry and classicism were transposed by Millet into the everyday life of the soil. It was a new kind of freedom as compared with the Romantic fantasy—freedom to depict the humble, the poor, the inarticulate, the inexpressive. Considered common and coarse by the critics, Millet's art became immensely popular. He revolutionized observation and direct expression. In his home at Barbizon on the outskirts of the Fontaine-bleau Forest, he gathered numerous disciples, although he taught none directly.

While Millet was patiently studying peasantry and filling his visions of the earth with the grace of a religious spirit, Courbet was chiefly interested in the depiction of the working classes with a view to social and political propaganda. Courbet was a fighter, his goal to portray with sincerity the everyday life of the workers. He was also a great landscape artist and a good animal painter; he abhorred historical scenes. He was noted for his pride, which was in a measure justified, for he made no concession whatever to public taste. Color he utterly sacrificed to value and form, and to expression of features and attitude. *The Burial at Ornans* displays these qualities at their best, yet it was ridiculed at the Salon of 1850, where his sincere rendering of the awkwardly solemn participants was thought to be almost caricature. The following year, *The Stone Breakers* suffered the same fate and was moreover thought "commonplace"; its marvelous truth of gesture and sobriety were quite overlooked. His revolutionary ideas took shape in his paintings of women, large, opulent and somewhat coarse bathers and working girls.

Courbet's powerful influence intermingled with other tendencies produced one of the foremost painters of the century, Édouard Manet. Courbet himself is sometimes considered a painter who did not quite fulfill himself, yet it cannot be denied that, although his Realism is tinged with Romanticism, in keeping with the novels of Zola and the whole trend of fashion at the time, he was the first to brush away the false sentiment of Romanticism and thus pave the way to a modern outlook on art.

Daumier, the friend of Corot and Courbet's fellow-realist, was at first

THÉODORE ROUSSEAU.—Evening, or The Vicar (detail). Toledo, Arthur J. Sécor Collection.

Théodore Rousseau is the painter of trees; no other artist has been able to express better than he the restless force of great oaks. Those which are seen in this landscape of Berri have retained during winter their foliage reddened by autumn.

DELACROIX.—The Massacres of Scio. Paris, Musée du Louvre.

DELACROIX.—The Battle of Taillebourg (detail). Museum of Versailles.

Delacroix believed that the great events of the Middle Ages deserved to be glorified by painting just as much as those of antiquity, which were then the only subjects accepted by the classical artists.

DELACROIX.—July 28, 1830, or Liberty at the Barricades. Paris, Musée
du Louvre.

*An historical painter, Delacroix rarely depicted contemporary events; here he
glorifies the exaltation of the people during the Revolution of 1830 in which he
took part. The composition is Romantic; the insurgents come in a diagonal
line from the background of the picture; in the corpses of the foreground
Delacroix recalls the works of Gros.*

chiefly famous as a caricaturist whose caustic pen created types truer than
life itself. Towards the end of his career, he painted a number of striking
pictures in which he used to the utmost his uncanny power of suggesting
by means of a few simple, concentrated strokes. In canvases such as
The Pit or *The Third-Class Carriage*, it becomes plain that Daumier's brush
depicted people as they really are. Reminiscent of Goya, his art has
something Spanish in its heroic violence.

INGRES.—The Grand Odalisque.   Paris, Musée du Louvre.

Painted in Rome, this "odalisque" indicates a reminiscence of Raphael (portrait of the Fornarina) and Titian (Venus of Urbino), but it was also inspired by ancient cameos.   Ingres plays lightly with anatomical realities in order to obtain a graceful form and an elegant arabesque.

INGRES.—Mademoiselle Rivière.   Paris, Musée du Louvre.

The frail grace of this young girl of fifteen is all the more touching when it is known that she died the following year.

INGRES.—Monsieur Bertin.   Paris, Musée du Louvre.

In this picture, where realism dominates Ingres' customary idealism, the painter has left an unforgettable figure of the power of the 19th century bourgeoisie, so sure of itself, and still close to the vigor of the more humble classes.

J.-F. MILLET.—The Gleaners.   Paris, Musée du Louvre.

Going beyond the effort of Romanticism, Millet, who was himself a peasant, affirmed that the most humble activities of country-life had the grandeur of the most heroic actions.   Settled at Barbizon in 1848, on the edge of the forest of Fontainebleau, he painted the country chores in the wheat fields of Brie.   However, the stiff gestures of these gleaners and the isolated figures of the composition indicate that Millet, although he was self-taught, did not break cleanly with Classicism.   The landscape, enveloped in the warm, blond clearness of summer, is one of the most beautiful that he ever painted.

Daumier is inseparable from his period, that of the rising bourgeoisie, the growth of Parliamentarism, the deep artistic and social unrest between 1830 and 1852.   He pinned down with pen and brush the foibles and villainies of his day—the snobs, the swaggerers, the politicians, the bankers, in all their self-complacency.   Yet he often relaxed in tender, whimsical compositions such as *The Painter* or *The Print-Lover* indulging their beloved

COROT.—Little Robert with a Trumpet.   Paris, Musée du Louvre.

As well as a landscape artist, Corot is a fine portraitist who likes simple models—parents, humble folk, and unsophisticated children—with whom his guileless spirit finds something in common.

hobbies, or *The Washerwoman*, helping a little child up wet and slippery steps.

Perhaps as an unconscious reaction against Realism, we find in France as elsewhere in Europe the simultaneous development of idealistic art which, however, partakes of the truculence and force of the Realists. Monticelli is the painter of color for its own sake, laid on the canvas in thick, rough, tapestry-like effects to give life to phantoms in a fantastic world. His opposite is Carrière whose colorless, shadowy manner, just on the verge of reality, makes us see his vision as through the mist of our own emotion. Henner is the poet of suggestion, while Odilon Redon, in the ghostly radiance of evanescent color, seems to be wafted into the beyond. Such art has often been criticized for its Romantic conventionality and evasive technique, yet most of these painters advanced artistic expression.

The origin of Impressionism may be found in various aspects of the work of painters as widely different as Velasquez and Constable, Frans Hals and Corot, Watteau, Vermeer and Turner. While Classicism prevailed, it was difficult to develop interest in light, and its effects remained of secondary importance. Once Romanticism had set the artist's inspiration free, it became increasingly possible to experiment with subjects and techniques of every nature.

Scientific discovery also played a part in the movement. In 1839, Chevreul, a French scientist to whom are due a great many discoveries in the chemical and dyeing industries, published a treatise dealing with his research in the domain of color. He proved scientifically what had been empirically known as far back as Watteau, namely that primary colors, not mixed but merely set side by side in minute touches, give the effect of their composite color to the eye when viewed at a certain distance. The color thus created is much purer than it would be if mixed on the palette. Infinite variations may be obtained by placing the touches in different proportions or adding minute specks of other colors to give a cooler or a warmer tint. Although the influence of Chevreul's theories was not felt before Seurat, still the new school of painters then working under the spiritual guidance of Corot, Millet, Daubigny and the other Barbizon artists, was quick to seize the possibility of methodically rendering the truth they had sought by instinct and sometimes found by chance. In a quiet, unobtrusive way, painters like Jongkind and Boudin had already tried to render exactly what they saw and to translate the evanescent radiance of sea and sky without making a method of their attempts.

Boudin lived at Le Havre; he was an admirer of Millet and, after a fruitless period of study in Paris, was in despair at having wasted his time and achieved so little at the age of 30. Strolling idly along one day, he noticed in a shop window several paintings done in an inexperienced manner

J.-F. Millet.—The Rainbow.   Paris, Musée du Louvre.

Millet's best paintings are perhaps his landscapes.   Here, he has captured the brief moment after the storm when the rainbow suddenly brightens a landscape still sparkling with rain.

DAUBIGNY.—Fishing. Private Collection.

Daubigny still uses the dull tones and the opaque greens of the Romantics; but contrary to the latter, who were attached to the soil, he preferred the rivers and their early morning mists. He even had a studio-boat built so that he might work on the Oise; he thus foreshadows the Romantic sensibility of Fantin-Latour.

he found congenial and whose author he discovered to be a boy of 16, Claude Monet. The friendship thus formed between the two lasted a lifetime and brought a great change in the history of painting.

Boudin taught the lad a new thing, a fad of his own which few other painters shared: the pursuit of nature out of doors. No need for a studio with elaborate hangings and plaster casts; a portable easel and a box of paints was all an artist required. After three years spent on the cliffs of Normandy in the company of Boudin and Jongkind, small wonder that Monet could hardly bring himself to settle down in the stuffy Paris studio

COURBET.—The Burial at Ornans (detail).   Paris, Musée du Louvre.

At the Salon of 1851 this picture produced a veritable scandal.   One imbecile wrote that "being buried at Ornans was enough to disgust a person."   Courbet has painted with realism a village burial where humor mingles with indifference, grief and pathos.

COROT.—The Cathedral of Chartres. Paris, Musée du Louvre.

*As Constable had already done in England, Corot liked to use medieval
monuments, churches or châteaux, as subjects for his canvases.*

COURBET.—The Stone Breakers. Museum of Dresden.

Whereas Millet painted the chores of the country, it was the work of the laborer that interested Courbet. As a Socialist, he saw in the worker an indication of the proletariat, victim of the new-born industrial civilization. The humble task of the stone breaker is for him a symbol of that misery.

of Gleyre, where he went to acquire a classical training in spite of his longing for the air and light of Daubigny's landscapes.

In 1863, upon closer acquaintance with a fellow-student at the Gleyre Academy, a youth uncultured and innocent in his approach to art whose name was Auguste Renoir, Monet found that their aims were similar and that it was useless to waste time at Gleyre's. The young men were joined by other students who felt similarly lost at the academy: Alfred Sisley, whose particular gift as a landscape painter was due perhaps to his British origin, and Frédéric Bazille, an unusually talented young man killed in the war of 1870, before he had fulfilled himself. The four decided to leave Gleyre and strike out on their own.

Another group had come together at the Académie Suisse; it included the Provençal Cézanne, Camille Pissarro, who had just arrived from the West Indies and was enthralled by Corot, and Armand Guillaumin. The

COURBET.—The Young Ladies of the Seine.   Museum of Fine Arts
of the City of Paris.

*Odd because of its subject, which is an attempt at social satire, this picture is
one of the most beautiful works in all of Courbet's painting.*

DAUMIER.—Don Quixote in the Mountain.   Robert Freat Payne Collection.

In his numerous drawings, watercolors, and paintings which illustrate the story of Don Quixote, Daumier expressed in his own way the feeling of disillusion that deeply troubled the Romantic souls.

DAUMIER.—The Print-lover (detail).   Paris, Longa Collection.

Daumier, who was self-taught and who started to paint at a late date, proceeded ardently, superposing his paints in a manner that well expressed the violence of his temperament.

CHASSÉRIAU.—Peace (detail).   Decoration of the Cour des Comptes.
Paris, Musée du Louvre.

Chassériau accomplished his masterpiece in the fresco paintings that decorated the great Staircase of the Cour des Comptes. They formed the most beautiful monumental work of the century, but were unfortunately almost entirely destroyed in the fire set by the Communards in 1871.

PUVIS DE CHAVANNES.—Ave Picardia Nutrix (detail).   Museum of Amiens.

The monumental effort of Puvis de Chavannes goes back to Ingres, and even more to the paintings of Chassériau at the Cour des Comptes.   At the height of the Impressionist period, he prolonged the spirit of Classicism.

FANTIN-LATOUR.—The Atelier of Batignolles.   Paris, Musée du Louvre.

Around Manet, shown seated painting at his easel, are grouped from left to right several habitués of the gatherings at the Café Guerbois: the German painter Otto Schœlderer (behind the artist), Renoir with his hat on, Emile Zola, Edmond Maitre, the painter Bazille, and in the rear Monet.

two groups soon became acquainted through Pissarro who knew Monet.

The world of art was then severely criticizing a rising young painter, Edouard Manet, whose daring *Déjeuner sur l'herbe* had been rejected by the Salon of 1863.   Although inspired by Raphael, this composition was considered impossible, chiefly because the setting was not antique and the men were depicted in everyday attire alongside female bathers in the nude. Manet and a group of other painters, rejected for various reasons (among them Whistler, Fantin-Latour and young Pissarro) were permitted to exhibit, by special favor of Napoleon III, in a separate enclosure.   The success of the Salon des Refusés was unparalleled; the battle between official and unofficial art was raging again as in the heroic days of Romanticism.

The older and the younger group of rebels, introduced to each other by Zola and Pissarro, found much in common, though at first their aims were different. For a long time they met regularly at the Café Guerbois where they discussed painting and literature, and taught each other more than any academy could have done. In the atmosphere of intellectual fever which reigned here, they met the poets and writers of the day: Baudelaire, whom a narrow-minded tribunal had condemned in 1857 for his "Fleurs du Mal," the cryptic Stéphane Mallarmé, the brilliant Théophile Gautier, Verlaine and Rimbaud the outlaws, Alphonse Daudet, Théodore de Banville, the Goncourt Brothers and Emile Zola. They were often joined by the aristocratic Degas and the Belgian painter of Parisian elegance, Alfred Stevens. Often Zola brought a shy, silent young man, his friend Cézanne, who did not hold quite the same views.

Fantin-Latour made several group portraits of his friends in almost classic style; we know how they looked, their favorite attitudes, almost their very thoughts. When summer came, they did not separate as is the wont of fellow-artists or students in Paris. They went to work in the forest, near Fontainebleau and Barbizon, where they lodged in rustic inns or camped out in the open. There they met Diaz, Rousseau and Millet.

In 1865, which may be considered the peak of the century, one of the peaceful, prosperous years before the conflict, there were three groups, three generations working in sympathy with each other and representing the evolution of modern art. Of the eldest group, Millet was the leader. He was just over 50 and had not quite attained his subsequent fame. Rousseau was 53, Dupré a year older, Diaz, the eldest, 58, while Daubigny was just 10 years younger than the latter. They lived in dire poverty and voluntary seclusion, suffering many a rebuff from the public and the official artists.

The second group, headed by Manet, was fighting its hardest battles. After the refusal of the *Déjeuner sur l'herbe*, Manet undaunted struck hard again with *Olympia*, exhibited in 1865. The picture excited the most adverse criticism. Although here again he was copying the classic Titian and Goya, the realism of the nude, its unacademic surroundings, its Baudelairian atmosphere of lazy vice, the modern, impudent air of the young woman, the Negress, the cat and its paw-marks on the sheet, even the just-bought flowers in their crinkly paper, scandalized the critics to the utmost. *Olympia* entered the Louvre about 30 years later, after Claude Monet had organized a subscription to buy it from the master's widow.

Claude Monet was the leader of the youngest group which included

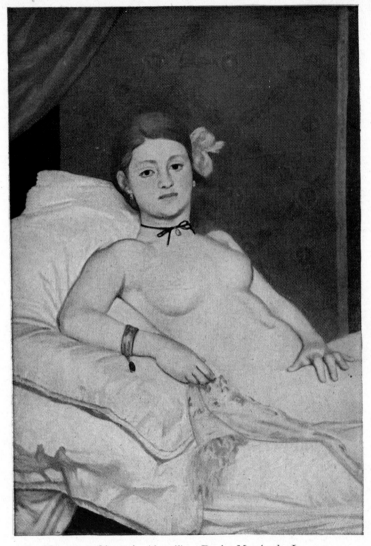

MANET.—Olympia (detail).   Paris, Musée du Louvre.

*This realistic conception of a nude, which was opposed to the "academic"
conventions judged indispensable for this type of painting, produced a scandal
at the Salon of 1864.*

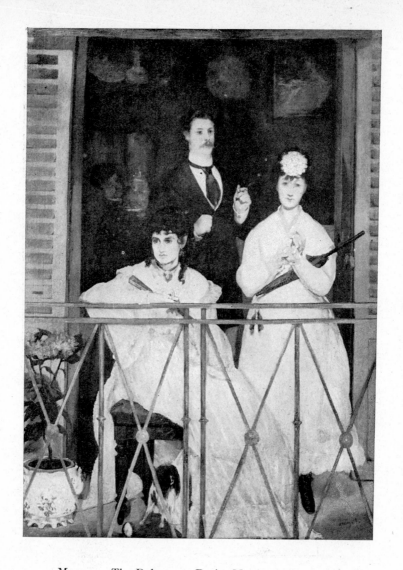

MANET.—The Balcony.   Paris, Musée du Louvre.

*Manet perhaps borrowed from Goya the idea of painting figures appearing
on a balcony.   The woman seated in the foreground is Berthe Morisot, Manet's
sister-in-law, who was also his pupil.*

MANET.—The Fifer. Paris, Musée du Louvre.
In this silhouette presented against a plain background, in these simplified tones and broad technique, Manet evidently remembers Velazquez.

MANET.—"Le Déjeuner sur l'herbe," or "The Picnic" (detail). Paris, Musée du Louvre. *The Naturalism of this picture caused a tremendous scandal at the Salon des Refusés of 1863. It is a transposition of one of Raphael's works which was known through an engraving by Marc-Antoine.*

MANET.—"Le Bon Bock." Philadelphia, Carroll Tyson Collection.

For this picture, which was painted upon his return from a trip to Holland, and which enjoyed considerable success at the Salon of 1873, Manet draws his inspiration from Frans Hals. A critic said that the subject "was drinking Haarlem beer."

MANET.—Still-Life with Brioche.   Glasgow, Leonard Gow Collection.

Manet's still-lifes are his most delightful canvases.   In painting before the 20th century, the human figure always more or less restrained the artist; in still-lifes the painter found more freedom for his research in composition and technique.

Renoir, Sisley, Pissarro.   Later on, they were joined by two charming young women. Berthe Morisot, a pupil of Manet, whose delicate still-lifes and tender harmonies show much of the emotion of Corot, married her teacher's brother.   Mary Cassatt never married, yet no painter has had a more exquisite insight into the eternal theme of the mother and child.

The first encounter of Manet and Monet was not precisely a friendly one. Manet noticed the young man's signature on *The Lady in Green*, exhibited in 1866.   He was somewhat disgruntled because his own *Fifer* had been

BOUDIN.—Entrance to the Port of Le Havre.   Denver Art Museum.

A native of Le Havre, Boudin was, with Jongkind, the real forerunner of Impressionism.   It was he who lead the young Claude Monet to paint in the open air.   He was essentially a painter of nautical surroundings.

rejected at the same Salon and thought Monet was taking advantage of the similarity in name to gain notoriety.   In spite of this, they became great friends.

The influence of Monet and his circle, especially of Berthe Morisot, and also undoubtedly Manet's inherent eye for color and light, by degrees made the painter of Olympia take up the new manner.   As the years went by, his work became more and more Impressionistic.   He was the link between Realism and Impressionism because he practised both and finally forsook the one for the other; in this sense he may be considered the first of the modern painters.

Manet's contemporary Degas had deserted Neo-Classicism and struck out on his own in a manner neither wholly Realistic nor yet Impressionistic. He did not worship color; his aim was to depict movement, gesture and expression.   He showed little sympathy with, but rather a scientific interest

CAILLEBOTTE.—The Floor Waxers.   Paris, Musée du Louvre.

Financially better-off than his friends the Impressionists, Caillebotte helped them a great deal by buying their canvases and thus formed a collection which he later bequeathed to the State. In his own works he sometimes imitated Monet, but seems to have been more interested than he in the problems of the human figure. His art remains tinged with Naturalism, and this picture might be one of Courbet's, if the light which gleams on the flooring did not indicate a new kind of research.

in, the lower classes from which he chose his models. Far less sociable than his friends, he resembled in this Cézanne. In spite of his desire for solitude, he often came to the Café Guerbois, and so great was his interest in the rising young school that he helped them organize their first great exhibition which earned their endeavor the name of Impressionism.

The exhibition was held in 1874 on the premises of Nadar, the famous photographer. There were about 30 artists, among whom Monet, Degas, Boudin, Renoir, Sisley, Pissarro, Berthe Morisot, Guillaumin and Cézanne

BAZILLE.—Family Gathering (detail).   Paris, Musée du Louvre.

Bazille shows the members of his own family gathered on the terrace of his home at Meru, near Montpellier.   In the background of the picture shines the harsh light of the "Midi," rather than the more delicate tones of the "Ile-de-France."

MONET.—Westminster. Paris, Musée du Louvre.

The influence of Turner, whose works Monet had seen in London in 1871, did not become evident until the painter's maturity. Then he went back to the Thames to paint the flickering light of the great port with its foggy, smoky atmosphere.

were singled out for future fame. Among them, too, was Caillebotte, a painter of talent and an enthusiastic amateur who helped his friends by purchasing their canvases, which he later bequeathed to the nation. Monet exhibited five pictures, one of which happened to be called *Impression: Soleil levant.* It must not be forgotten that during the war of 1870 Monet had visited London, where he had had the opportunity of studying the

MONET.—Tulip Field in Holland (detail). Paris, Musée du Louvre.

Monet sojourned in Holland for the first time in 1871, and then especially was attracted by the canals. On his second trip in 1886, Monet, far more enthusiastic about the exaltation of color, used the tulip fields as subject for his works.

MONET.—The Embroiderer. Private Collection.

Monet rarely painted figures. They almost all date from his first period, after 1870. Later, the figures faded, drowned by the light.

SISLEY.—St. Mammès, A Grey Day. Boston, Museum of Fine Arts.

More of a traditionalist than Monet, Sisley most often maintains perspective in his compositions by using rivers, canals, or village streets as his subjects.

works of Turner and Constable. The title of the picture sounds much like Turner in his most evanescent mood. The critics seized upon it, and in a very witty article the subject and its title were so amusingly derided that the name of "Impressionist" was applied to the whole group. As they found it apt enough, it remained. It characterizes the manner as no other word can do. For its essence was the art of seizing a fleeting impression, a vision as immaterial and instantaneous as the emotion felt by Corot in the dewy dawn. The impression changes with the point of view, the season, the time of day, the weather, the mood of the sun. It has nothing to do with the subjective thoughts of the artist, his memories or his dreams. It was pure objective vision.

SISLEY.—A Street at Rouen.   Private Collection.
Here the perspective is well centered on the steeple.

ALFRED SISLEY.—Floods at Port-Marly (detail).   Paris, Louvre.

Sisley never tired of the poetry of the Ile-de-France.   His art recalls something of the sensitive feeling of Corot.

PISSARRO.—The Market at Pontoise. Gallery of Art, Kansas City, Mo·
*Settled at Pontoise, Pissarro, following the example of Jean-François Millet,
was interested in scenes of peasant life and country chores; he was the most
"rustic" of the Impressionists.*

PISSARRO.—Little Peasant Girl Seated (detail).　Paris, Musée du Louvre.

PISSARRO.—The Road at Louveciennes. Paris, Musée du Louvre.
Pissarro often painted the grey and blue melancholy of the winter country-side.

The Impressionist manner was finally recognized even by officials who had disdained it; about 1880 the luminous style won its way into the painting of the Salon. However, it is interesting to note that Cézanne was still held in contempt; after his failure at the second Impressionist exhibition in 1876, he ceased to show his paintings until 1895.

Impressionism left no artist indifferent. It was not a question of fashion, as the critics of the time complained. The artist and the art-lover merely became aware of the truth of light, air and color, and the old manner of painting became as obsolete as plain chant in the age of harmony.

Renoir delighted in the feminine form. With his love of color, he

BERTHE MORISOT.—Two Young Girls. Washington, D. C.,
Phillips Memorial Gallery.

*At first a pupil of Corot, and then of Manet her brother-in-law, Berthe Morisot
later imitated Renoir. It is Manet's influence which is most evident here.*

RENOIR.—The Washerwomen. Private Collection.

*It is by his technique of painting in transparent layers that Renoir obtains
that same iridescent quality of tone that Rubens had achieved before him.*

RENOIR.—"Le Moulin de la Galette." Paris, Musée du Louvre.

This picture was almost entirely painted at the "Moulin de la Galette," a Montmartre amusement spot where the artists of the time used to gather; it was in fact from that period that dated the vogue of Montmartre as an artists' center. The luscious flesh-tints and the silky dresses shimmer in the warm half-light of a beautiful summer afternoon.

reconciled a deep admiration for the purity of Ingres; in his *Bathers* the beauty of line is equal to the radiance of the flesh. His women are graceful yet opulent creatures like the women of Rubens, but without their Flemish solidity, at least in his first manner; they are Frenchwomen, supple and small-boned, and there is something eternally childlike and trusting in their full lips and heavy eyelids. He excelled in the rendering of sunlight falling through foliage on happy crowds, above all he was a painter of happiness. No social problems worried him. He worked without effort, rubbing layer after layer of transparent paint on his canvases until his vision shone

Auguste Renoir.—Gabrielle With a Rose (detail).　Paris, Louvre.

Renoir called this canvas «Gabrielle», from the name of the servant who acted as his model.　He delighted in the feminine form.　With his love of color, he showed a deep admiration for the beauty of line and the radiance of the flesh.

RENOIR.—Girl Combing her Hair.   Private Collection.

*In this picture from his so-called "nacreous" period, Renoir enjoys painting
the milky transparency of the flesh-tints which he sets off by the green tones of
the leaves and the brilliance of the materials.*

DEGAS.—After the Bath.   Private Collection.

Compared to the preceding picture by Renoir, this nude shows clearly that Degas' personality is less inclined toward beauty than toward seeking a life-like attitude and the analysis of movement.

through as though evoked by magic. He considered his painting finished when the flesh looked pleasant to touch.

This joy of creating was not granted to all the Impressionists. Among them, yet not of them, having neither facility nor their carefree attitude, we find the violent individuality of Paul Cézanne.

Cézanne, from the first, was a rebel, although a loyal one. He exhibited with his friends and bore his share of sarcasm, yet his main object was not the rendering of light so much as the creation of volume by means of well-defined planes and precise outlines. He strove to restore to landscape the solid architecture of Classicism, but by taking its principles from nature itself and not from school recipes. That is what he called "re-creating Poussin after nature."

While others struggled to make themselves known and appreciated, Cézanne's battles were with himself. He sometimes spent ten years on a picture, only to destroy it in despair. Not the least of his merits is his realism in still-life painting. He was the first to see beauty in the humblest objects set with no apparent pre-arrangement upon a plain cloth. Like Turner, he lived solely for his art, caring for nothing else and utterly oblivious of himself.

Cézanne already leads us out of Impressionism. Between 1880 and 1890, several movements were to react against the surrender to pure sensation, which is Impressionism, and to reinstate intellectual inspiration in art. The movement called Neo-Impressionism or Divisionism, definitely inspired by the theories of Chevreul, proposed to introduce method into the analysis of luminous phenomena and their plastic expression. Applying literally the principle of the composition of colors, the Neo-Impressionists painted by means of little patches of color set side by side and intended to give at a distance the impression of the desired tone. This movement arose in 1886 and did not last long; when its leader Seurat died in 1891, Pissarro joined it for a while, but only Signac remained faithful to it until our times.

How can the reaction against Impressionism be explained, considering the struggles of the movement to establish itself and its short period of supremacy? It seems that every movement, however revolutionary, tends to crystallize into a school and a tradition, and becomes in the eyes of the younger generation an "academism" to be overthrown. Cézanne became the black sheep of the fold while the movement was yet in its infancy because he sensed further possibilities of which his contemporaries were as yet unaware.

The development of Post-Impressionism was greatly favored by the growth of the Symbolist movement in literature. Verlaine, Rimbaud and Mallarmé, the leaders of the school, delighted in subtle, almost cryptic

DEGAS.—Dancers (detail).   Pastel.   Toledo Museum of Art.
It is in his pastels that Degas has best displayed his qualities as a colorist.

DEGAS.—After the Bath (detail). Paris, Ambroise Vollard Collection.

Degas provided outstanding innovations by his disarticulated compositions, his off-centre perspectives, and his unusual "shots" which foreshadow those of the movies. All that permitted him to grasp life in its most original moments.

CÉZANNE.—Still-Life. Boston, Museum of Fine Arts.

In his still-lifes Cézanne seeks to resolve the problems of construction, and he reduces his objects to their geometrical principles ; this still-life icould be considered as a study on the theme of the sphere.

shades of meaning. They carried into effect Baudelaire's conception of unity between the various artistic expressions; thus painters and composers such as Debussy participated in the movement and brought to life new and startling theories.

While Seurat and Signac were practising Divisionism and Cézanne striving to express volumes and planes by means of color alone, other painters, some of them contemporaries who had found their vocation late in life, came to the fore. Of these the most striking are Van Gogh and Gauguin.

Their lives have many strange points in common. Both started painting

CÉZANNE. Three Bathers. Paris, Petit Palais.

The rediscovery of the great principles of Classical composition, which allied the nude with Nature, was a problem that haunted Cézanne all his life and especially during his last years.

late and were almost self-taught, both were unbalanced and unhappy. But while Van Gogh led a lonely, frustrated life, full of misgivings and torment that drove him to suicide, Gauguin fulfilled himself in every respect, being a born fighter. Their work is symbolic of their natures.

Cézanne.—Portrait of Gustave Geoffroy. Paris,
Lecomte-Pellerin Collection.

Everything in this unfinished composition gives the impression of solidity and
elementary force. Cézanne endows this man of letters with the burliness of a
peasant.

CÉZANNE.—The Village of Cergy near Pontoise. Paris, Private Collection.

SEURAT.—The Grande Jatte. Chicago Art Institute.

Exhibited at the Salon des Indépendants of 1886, this picture had demanded of Seurat a long and patient effort, and it was so to speak the manifesto of Neo-Impressionism.

CÉZANNE.—Young Man with the Red Vest.　Zurich, Private Collection.

Cézanne was striving to record the different realities, the permanent form and color of each subject and each expression in a face.

SIGNAC.—Ships. Private Collection.

Both attached meanings to colors, yellow being dear to Van Gogh.

Gauguin's strong personality attracted a number of young artists to his retreat at Pont-Aven, Brittany. Of these disciples, the most interesting is Emile Bernard, who was the first to discover the power and beauty of painting in the manner of stained-glass windows and surrounding each color with a dark outline like the leads in the panels. Another enthusiast was Paul Sérusier, the theoretician of the group, through whom the discovery passed down to Maurice Denis and Pierre Bonnard, the Nabis.

The Nabis were very young when, about 1890, they chose this name, a Hebrew word meaning "prophets." They rejected academism, Realism

and even Impressionism, in spite of a certain regard for Monet and Renoir. Their recognized masters were Cézanne and Gauguin. Paul Séruzier and Maurice Denis were their leaders. The group consisted of five: Bonnard, Vuillard, Roussel, Ibels and Piot, to whom is sometimes added Ranson. Only the first three are widely known. They lead us into the 20th century. Maurice Denis was more directly inspired by the clear-cut style of Gauguin allied with the radiant art of the Italian primitives. He was the most religious of contemporary painters and strove to blend harmoniously the peacefulness of a Puvis with the rich, glowing color of the South Sea magician.

SEURAT.—The Channel of Gravelines (detail). Paris, Private Collection.
Seurat's landscapes are usually water scenes: views of the Seine or seascapes made in Normandy.

SEURAT.—"Le Chahut."   Buffalo, Albright Art Gallery.

This picture is rigorously constructed according to set principles; it is executed with the patient technique of "pointillism" which tends to rationalize the Impressionist discoveries concerning light.   Seurat's art does not wish to leave anything to chance.

VAN GOGH.—The Man with the Pipe (detail). Paul Rosenberg Collection.

This "man with the pipe" is none other than Van Gogh himself as he appeared, at Arles, after a fit of madness resulting from a dispute with Gauguin whom he had threated to kill. To punish himself he cut off an earlobe (the bandage is seen here). This picture is a sort of demonstration of pure coloring.

Van Gogh.—The Cypresses. Private Collection.

Van Gogh, with his ardent temperament, liked cypresses because of their trembling, flame-like undulation when whipped by the wind.

Van Gogh.—Flowers.   Bernheim-Jeune Collection.
*In his pictures of flowers Van Gogh finds a justification, furnished by Nature,
of his taste for exaggerated colors.*

GAUGUIN.—The Yellow Christ. Paul Rosenberg Collection.

In this work Gauguin returns voluntarily to primitive hieratism of which he found the example in Brittany; he thus protests against the Impressionists' submission to Nature.

GAUGUIN.—" La Belle Angèle " (detail).   Paris, Musée du Louvre.

Gauguin in his figure paintings always seemed to be seeking to record the
physical form in symbolic line and color.

GAUGUIN.—Merahi Metua no Tehamana: the Ancestors of Tehamana.
New York, Stephen Clark, Collection.

The live figure is hardly less hieratic than the Maori fetish placed behind it;
among the Polynesians of Tahiti, Gauguin rediscovered that primitive feeling
with which he had first come in contact when in Brittany.

GAUGUIN.—"L'Appel." George Wildenstein Collection.

FORAIN.—Portrait of the Countess Anna de Noailles. Private Collection.

Forain is more successful as a satiric draughtsman than as a painter. His works most worthy of interest are the portraits which fixed for posterity the features of certain celebrities at the end at the century.

TOULOUSE-LAUTREC.—At the Circus (detail). The Spanish Walk.
Knœdler Collection.

*Toulouse-Lautrec is above all a draftsman. Here he is interested in the
elegant arabesque formed by the silhouette of the horse and rider.*

TOULOUSE-LAUTREC.—Maxime Dethomas. Washington, D. C.,
National Gallery of Art.

*In draughtsman-like manner, Lautrec contrasts here the hard and somber
silhouette of the portrait with the filmy charm of the gowns in the background.*

TOULOUSE-LAUTREC.—"A la mie." Boston, Museum of Fine Arts.
Accentuating the Naturalism of Degas, Toulouse-Lautrec painted the moral decay of prostitutes and drunkards.

PAUL SÉRUSIER.—Landscape with Unicorns.   Private Collection.

A disciple of Gauguin, Paul Sérusier put his master's art into theory; in his paintings, Gauguin's forms are systematized and stylized.

MAURICE DENIS.—Homage to Cézanne. Paris, Museum of Modern Art.
This picture shows, gathered around a painting by Cézanne, from left to right: Redon, Vuillard, Mellerio, Maurice Denis, Sérusier, Ranson, Roussel, Bonnard and Mme Maurice Denis. This indicates that Cézanne was indeed "the father of contemporary art."

TOULOUSE-LAUTREC.—Miss May Belfort (detail).   Bernheim-Jeune Coll.
*Toulouse-Lautrec made himself the amused chronicler of the singers of the
"cafés-concerts," entertainment spots in vogue at the end of the century.*

PIERRE BONNARD.—The River Seine.   Private Collection.

*Bonnard's sensitive landscapes, his shimmering grisailles offer us, with a
new interpretation of the Impressionist movement, the vision of a serene and
peaceful world.*

PIERRE BONNARD.—Torso. Bernheim Jeune Collection.

PIERRE BONNARD.—Breakfast (detail).   Paris, Petit Palais.

While basing his works on the human figure, Bonnard has sought to blend his subjects intimately with the atmosphere in which they bathe.

BONINGTON.—View of Venice.   Paris, Musée du Louvre.

Bonington was the first of the landscape artists to transpose to oil painting the limpidness and fluidity of watercolors, a process cherished by the English since the 18th century.

ENGLAND

Englisch painting in the 19th century is marked by the continuation of the tradition of Hogarth, Reynolds and Gainsborough and, to an even greater degree, the development of new trends in the history of art.   The most important of these is landscape painting and the watercolor technique. The Pre-Raphaelite movement, though preceded by the Nazarene school in Germany, also became peculiarly English and grew into an important offshoot of Romanticism.   Later, English art gradually lost its national charactersitics and merged into the vast European movements of Impressionism and its successors.

LAWRENCE.—The King of Rome. Versailles Museum.

Receiving from the past the technical traditions of English painting, Lawrence accentuates his natural tendency toward elegance and grace, and creates an aristocratic, impersonal, and somewhat conventional type of portrait.

ETTY.—Study of a Nude. London, Adams Gallery.

Etty breaks with the mundane traditions of English painting and creates nudes with a realistic frankness which at times recalls Courbet.

J. CROME.—Wherries on the Yare.   Leeds Art Gallery.

In this landscape with its contorted trees, its somber clouds, and solid terrain, John Crome reveals his sources: the landscapes of Ruisdael and Hobbema.

In the first years of the century, English painters continued to paint portraits and historical scenes in the approved manner. Sir Thomas Lawrence's likenesses, though sometimes delightful, are extremely conventional. About 1850, Sir Lawrence Alma-Tadema was still drawing his inspiration from Greco-Roman history, producing works as noble as they are unreal. William Etty, a pupil of Lawrence, was perhaps the greatest colorist and one of the best painters of the nude the English school has known. His warmth and delicacy are almost Venetian and his inspiration is a compromise between Classicism and Realism.

Romanticism in English art was chiefly characterized by an ardent

CONSTABLE.—The Leaping Horse. London, Victoria and Albert Museum.

By his splashing of colors and his fragmented touch, Constable leads up to the future research of the Impressionists.

CONSTABLE.—The Watermill.   Private Collection.

The thick touch enhances the richness of the soil and foliage, the fluidity of the water, and the depth of the sky.

curiosity about nature which found expression in the development of land-scape painting. This was prepared as early as the end of the 18th century by the progress of painting in watercolor, which may be said to be the national art of England. The English discovered nature long before the French; many English landscape painters came to France to work at the mouth of the Seine and even in Paris; thus they exercised a stimulating influence over the French school. Delacroix was closely acquainted with

TURNER.—The Sun Rising Through Vapor. London, National Gallery.

A forerunner of the Impressionists, Turner preferred water to all the other elements; most of his paintings are seascapes.

Turner.—The Grand Canal in Venice. New York, Metropolitan Museum.

many of them: particularly the Fieldings and to a still greater extent Richard Parkes Bonington. The latter, who died at 27, lived in France and Italy, his oils representing landscapes in Paris, Normandy and Venice, are done in the watercolor manner.

John Crome is the originator of modern landscape painting. His truth to nature and sensitive treatment make him more than a successor of the great Dutch masters. Constable was the first to break away from convention in his treatment of foliage and sunlight. For some reason, perhaps because the darkening of oil paint had changed the true tones of the old masters, it was a rule that trees should be brown and foliage a dark olive. Constable saw no necessity to maintain such a tradition. He used bright green when he chose, to the horror of the critics. Moreover, he made a great discovery of whose far-reaching consequences he was unaware. It was that a color appears truer if composed of several shades. This was a step towards the Impressionist theory. Like Turner and the Impressionists, Constable loved the transient play of light. Painting from direct observation, he did not descend to minute rendering of detail but, like the Impressionists, suggested almost as much as he expressed. His paintings have unfortunately darkened like those of his predecessors; moreover the practice of seizing nature in the open had not yet been thought of, and Constable went no farther than the walls of his studio. His composition and sense of values make him comparable to many of the old masters he admired, and he may be considered a link between classic and modern painting. His exhibit at the Paris Salon of 1824 created a sensation in the French Romantic circles; Delacroix, after having seen the *Haywain,* repainted the background of his *Massacres of Scio.*

Landscape painting afforded a marvelous opportunity for the study of light. Turner, who was a poet guided by his imagination, reveled in it, dissolving everything in a brilliant glow. Yet he never thought of subordinating subject to light effect as did the Impressionists. He painted splendidly dramatic scenes which an excess of light renders somewhat obscure; his manner is best revealed in his landscapes. His influence was decisive on Claude Monet, who discovered his works during a visit to London in 1871.

Outside France, Romanticism took the form of a return to the Middle Ages. There were spontaneous outbreaks of mysticism; groups of painters shrinking from contact with a bourgeois and hostile world segregated themselves, even to the extent of forming communities. Such was the Pre-Raphaelite group in England which was organized about 1850.

Their forerunner and spiritual father was William Blake, a Romantic before his time. As early as the end of the 18th century, Blake practised a subjective and almost subconscious art in which he united poetic and graphic visions in engravings and watercolors of singular power and beauty.

The Pre-Raphaelite Brotherhood, whose members at first signed their works with the mysterious initials P. R. B. in addition to their name, originated in 1848 in the association of William Holman Hunt and John Everett Millais, aged 19 and 17 respectively. Their dreams were soon dynamized by Dante Gabriel Rossetti, a young poet and painter whose Italian descent made him the leaven of the calm English group. He was a pupil of Ford Madox Brown who joined the Brotherhood officially much later. Ruskin, who did much to defend the Pre-Raphaelites against adverse criticism, puts their aim as follows: "to paint things as they probably did look and happen, not as, by rules of art developed under Raphael, they might be supposed gracefully, deliciously or sublimely to have happened."

BLAKE.—David Delivered Out of Many Waters. London, Tate Gallery, Millbank.—*William Blake was an extraordinary precursor; as early as the end of the 18th century he conceived an art which found its source in dreams, long before the Pre-Raphaelites and the Symbolists.*

MILLAIS.—Hearts Are Trumps (detail). Private Collection.

D. G. ROSSETTI.—Bel Color. Private Collection.

This dreamy figure with its languid features is that of Rossetti's wife, who, during her brief lifetime, was the muse of Pre-Raphaelitism.

Millais attains great pathos by simple and effective technical means, but the ideas he put on canvas were not his own. He was the most skilful of the Brotherhood; however he lacked imagination and his later works are mere condescensions to public taste.

The gifted Dante Gabriel Rossetti carried Romanticism to extremes. When his beautiful wife, who inspired the Pre-Raphaelite type of woman, died of consumption he had the just-completed manuscript of a book of poems buried with her, a gesture as characteristic as that of having her grave opened seven years later to recover the manuscript and publish it.

Pre-Raphaelitism, reduced to its true proportions by the passage of time, appears to have fallen short of its aims. Yet the movement exercised a refreshing influence and it is also noteworthy for having revived an interest in decoration and applied arts, chiefly through the activity of William Morris. Alfred Stevens, also distinguished himself as a painter and decorator. In the meantime, George Frederick Watts painted fine portraits and allegories, true to the Venetian style. Most of his best works are mural decorations.

Genre painting was exceedingly popular in England. One of its finest and most interesting figures is Wilkie in his early works. His appropriate minuteness does not exclude breadth of style and his quaint Scots humor in nowise mars his psychological insight into the manners and customs of his country. He has been widely reproduced and imitated; a similar fate has overtaken Landseer whose dogs and deer have become conventional from being imitated by inferior artists.

During the latter part of the century, the influence of the French was felt in one of the most unconventional painters of the period, Frank Brangwyn. His work is as varied as it is powerful and full of rich, romantic color. He had a predilection for Oriental subjects and industrial scenes which he invested with the decorative qualities he inherited from the Pre-Raphaelites.

FORD MADOX BROWN.—Doctor Primrose and His Daughters (detail).
Manchester, City Art Gallery.

DAVID WILKIE.—Portrait of Thomas Daniell. Private Collection.
An energetic portrait, painted with a penetrating psychology rarely seen in English art which always yields too easily to mundanity.

ALFRED STEVENS.—Portrait of Mrs. Mary Ann Collmann.
London, National Gallery.

*The influence of Italian Renaissance painting is especially perceptible in this
work.*

WATTS.—Portrait of the Violinist Josef Joachim. Chicago,
Hutchinson Collection.

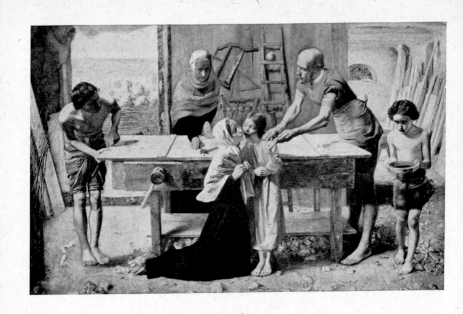

MILLAIS.—Christ in the House of His Parents. London,
Tate Gallery, Millbank.

In its quest for mystical expression, Pre-Raphaelitism set the fashion which consisted in an attempt to reconstruct historically scenes of the Gospel.

OTHER EUROPEAN COUNTRIES

IN comparison with the prodigious growth of art in France and England, the production of their neighbours in the 19th century shows a decline, particularly if we consider the past achievements of Italian and Spanish art.

There were no great painters in Belgium, where painting was bogged in the historical platitudes of Gallait and Wappers, the rhetoric of Charles le Groux, the Neo-Medieval realism of Leys and Braekeleer. The "Socialist" movement which affected Europe after 1850 produced in Belgium the popular art of Constantin Meunier, the bard of industrial life. A contemporary

JAMES ENSOR.—The Surprise of the Wouse Mask (detail). Antwerp Museum.
In Ensor's Expressionism, as early as 1880, are reborn the nightmares and dramatic violence of Jerome Bosch.

JAKOB MARIS.—Windmill.   Private Collection.

*Breaking away from tradition, Jakob Maris takes a new view of the Dutch
landscape; he was greatly helped in his work by his contact with the French
landscape artists of Barbizon.*

THYS MARIS.—The Cook.   Private Collection.

The vogue for the portrayal of ordinary people is one of the aspects of contemporary European painting after 1850.   This figure by the Dutch painter, Thys Maris, is reminiscent of Courbet, but with a certain Dutch placidity inherited from older Dutch painting.

Van Gogh.—The Potato Eaters (detail).   Amsterdam,
V. W. Van Gogh Collection.

During his "dark period," before joining with the Impressionists on his arrival
in Paris in 1885, Van Gogh belonged to the Dutch School.   And if he borrowed
from the masters of Paris their language of color, he nevertheless remained
very much aloof from the spirit which animated Impressionism; his sense of
prophecy and his passion for the great beyond ally him with the celebrated
Expressionist masters of the North, with Rembrandt and Albrecht Dürer.

JOSEF ISRAELS.—The Harp Player. Private Collection.
Forsaking historical subjects, Josef Israels tries to create a sort of humane and realistic Romanticism.

of the Impressionists, Alfred Stevens, expressed with a delicate brush though somewhat coldly the elegance of the Parisienne. Baertsoen, of Antwerp, painted fine landscapes of his native country. The innate artistic gifts of the Belgians were awakened in the 20th century, but as early as the end of the 19th James Ensor, ahead of all other Nordic or Germanic painters, accomplished the renaissance of Expressionism.

In Holland, the influence of the Barbizon School continued for a long

C. H. BREITNER.—Amsterdam's Landscape. Amsterdam, Rijkmuseum.

Like the French Impressionists, Breitner painted the variations of light according to the seasons. The canals of Amsterdam furnished him with a subject for study to which he remained faithful during his entire life.

ANTON MAUVE.—Homeward Bound.   Private Collection.

In Mauve's work, the feeling for Nature peculiar to the Dutch joins with the
atmospheric sensitivity of Corot and the earthy solidity of the masters of
Barbizon.

IGNACIO ZULOAGA.—Spanish Lady.   Private Collection.

By means of his hard line and earthy colors, the Spaniard Zuloaga seeks to emphasize the character of his models.

time in the works of Jakob and Thys Maris and of Anton Mauve, who gave
Van Gogh a few lessons; the latter also benefited, as may be seen in his
early "dark" manner, by the example of Josef Israels, the painter of popular
life. At the end of the century, Breither, a very fine landscape painter,
depicted the canals of Amsterdam in a colorful and spirited manner.
Holland on the whole lost her greatest painter, Vincent Van Gogh, who
became a part of the French School.

Spain continued the tradition of Goya, who died in 1828, with the
portraits of Vicente Lopez and the dramatic scenes of Eugenio Lucas.
Fortuny adapted Goya's inspiration to the more colorful manner of 1860.
At the end of the century, Ignacio Zuloaga attempted to renew the

VASSILI VERESTCHAGIN.—Monks at the Door of a Mosque, Turkestan.
Private Collection. *Many European painters at the end of the 19th century
followed the æsthetic tradition which relegated painting to the role of repro-
ducing reality with the greatest exactness.*

PIOTR MICHALOWSKY.—Work Horses. Museum of Varsouv.

The Polish painter, Michalowsky, is one of those rare European artists who has been able to adapt a romantic style to his own form of expression.   Hundreds of his paintings have been taken for works of Delacroix.

17th century traditions in a bold style which tended, like the greater part of 20th century European painting, towards Expressionism.

The Central European countries awakened to a Romanticism which drew its inspiration from national history, but expressed itself in purely realistic fashion. The most gifted in a pictorial sense was perhaps Michalovsky, a Pole whose manner was related to that of Géricault and Delacroix. In Hungary, Michael Munkacsy, a vigorous painter of Hungarian and Parisian life, changed from the old, dark manner of the classics to the luminous treatment of the open-air school. In Russia, the much

JOHANN FRIEDRICH OVERBECK.—Vittoria Coldoni. Museum of Munich.
This young peasant girl from the Roman country-side has been depicted by Overbeck with an idealization that draws its principles from the art of Raphael.

PHILIPP OTTO RUNGE.—The Flight into Egypt.   Hamburg, Runsthalle.

The Neo-Classical tendencies of Runge are opposed somewhat by an instinct for expression which he draws from the Germanic tradition.   The influence of Dürer is perceptible here.

traveled Vassili Verestchagin rendered in a realistic manner scenes from the Russo-Turkish war and observation made in India and Palestine.

In Germany, the Nazarenes with Overbeck and Cornelius, who worked together in Rome at the Convent of San Isidoro in 1810, showed the way to the Pre-Raphaelites in an attempt to go back to mediaeval times. Cornelius sought to rival Michelangelo in a monumental *Last Judgment* at Munich, while among his more gifted countrymen were Rethel, who decorated the Town Hall of Aix-la-Chapelle and Schwind, in his youth a book illustrator, who brought his whimsical touch to the decoration of the Vienna Opera House.   Free from all theory, the portrait-painter Philipp

CASPAR DAVID FRIEDRICH.—Landscape. Museum of Berlin.

A medieval ruin, lost in the depths of a legendary forest devastated by winter —truly a Romantic subject, but painted with a sort of eager attention to detail worthy of a Primitive.

Otto Runge, "the German David," was a virile and sincere realist. The landscape school developed a painter with the minute vision of Van Eyck, Caspar David Friedrich.

The schools of Düsseldorf and Munich had a great influence upon European and American art, not only on account of the personality of Schadow, a noted teacher, but also because of the Romantic atmosphere and the gay student life peculiar to Germany. Another noteworthy German painter was Schnorr von Carolsfeld who decorated the palace of King Ludwig of Bavaria with scenes from the *Nibelungenlied* and also designed stained-glass windows for St. Paul's in London. Adolf Menzel depicted with great skill a somewhat stiff and conventional way of life, as

JULIUS SCHNORR VON CAROLSFELD.—Frau von Quandt.   Museum of Munich.

This painting is a remarkable example of the authority exerted on the German School of the 19th century by the influence of the Italian Renaissance masters, especially Raphael.

WILHELM LEIBL.—The Critic. Private Collection.

Anselm von Lenbach.—Richard Wagner (detail). Private Collection.

In the art of portraiture, which had until then been permeated with romantic Expressionism, Lenbach introduced an entirely new realistic candor.

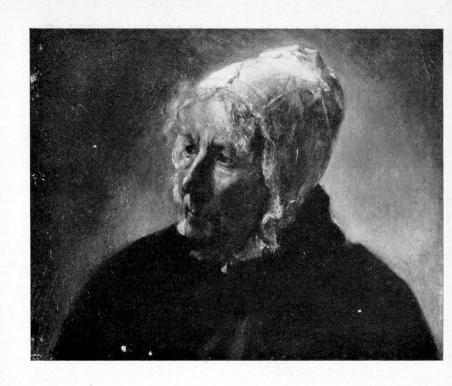

ADOLPH MENZEL.—Old Woman. Bonn, Kunsthistoris hes Institute.

*Menzel is one of the German painters who come under the influence of Courbet's
powerful realism.*

observed in the days of Frederick the Great and Wilhelm I. The influence
of Courbet, prevalent in Munich, inspired the realistic subjects of Wilhelm
Leibl. Impressionism penetrated into Germany with Anselm von Lenbach
and Max Liebermann, while Max Slevogt guided it towards Expressionism
which in the 20th century became the national German style. Charles
Munch, a Norwegian whose position is similar to that of Slevogt, was to
exercise a great influence over the destiny of German art.

Switzerland developed an extremely rich school of painting. In the

Max Liebermann.—Yard of the Orphans' Home in Amsterdam.

While remaining attatched to realistic subjects, Max Liebermann introduced into Germany the sketchy treatment and the luminous color of Impressionism.

early days of the century, Leopold Robert, a pupil of David, won local fame for his classical rendering of popular life in Italy. Charles Gleyre, a painter of portraits and historical scenes in the Neo-Classical manner, is famous for his pupils, Whistler, Renoir, Monet, Sisley. Barthélemy Menn and Alexandre Calame returned to nature, painting Alpine scenery in a style that remained Neo-Classic. The treatment of Frank Buchser, a contemporary of the Impressionists, was more modern; his travels in Spain, Morocco, the U. S. A. and other countries developed his vision and broadened his manner.

Max Slevogt.—Landscape. Frankfurt, Old Nathan Collection.

An imitator of Manet, Slevogt interprets Impressionism with a violence that betrays the dramatic temperament of his Germanic soul.

The greatest Swiss painter is Arnold Böcklin. He worked in Munich and in Italy; his poetic genius and vast imagination do not, however, allow us to forget his banal draughtsmanship and crude color. Obsessed by the idea of subordinating painting to thought, in the Pre-Raphaelite manner, he developed a personal style in which he attempted to mingle mythological and fanciful subjects with realistic form and the bright, luminous color of the Impressionists. Ferdinand Hodler rid painting of such literary pretences and drew his inspiration from the landscapes and the history

LEOPOLD ROBERT.—Young Girl from Sorrento.   Museum of Neuchatel.

*In his taste for Italian folklore, the Swiss painter Leopold Robert is romantic ;
but his style of painting remains classic.   Does not this young peasant girl
from Sorrento derive her beauty from a Madonna by Raphael?*

CHARLES GLEYRE.—The Bath. Lausanne, Museum of Fine Arts.

Academism tinged with realism: such was the position of Gleyre, who had a great number of students both in Switzerland and Paris.

ARNOLD BÖCKLIN.—Portrait of his Daughter Lucia.   Museum of Basel.

Böcklin wished to dissipate the heavy atmosphere of realism which was stifling German art; he drew his inspiration from legends and mythology; but his vision remained realistic and his craftsmanship was faithful to Classical procedures. Thus, the result of his art is ambiguous.

JOHANN HEINRICH FÜSSLI.—Titania Kissing Bottom.   Museum of Zurich.

A contemporary of William Blake, the Swiss Füssli, who incidentally worked in England, was one of the first artists to seek evasion in the domain of the symbol, the legend, the fantastic.

FERDINAND HODLER.—The Retreat of the Swiss at Marignan.   Museum
of Berne.

*In painting the epic of these Swiss soldiers of the Renaissance, who were sought
by all the armies of Europe, Hodler draws his inspiration from two artists
called the "lansquenet painters" Nicholas Manuel Deutsch and Urs Graf.
This taste for brutal energy opens the 20th century which was to be a century of
dramatic events.*

of his country.   The dramatic sense of the old 16th century Swiss painters,
Manuel Deutsch and Urs Graf, revives in Hodler's historical scenes.

The development of art in Europe, outside England and France, shows
the same tendency.   The Romantic movement gave Europe only its subjects, not the technique, which was invented by England and France.
The historical compositions of Romanticism were expressed in a realistic
manner, with reminiscences of the primitives in Germany.   In France the
same tendency existed side by side with pictorial Romanticism.   About
1860, contemporary themes appear.

John Vanderlyn.—Ariadne. Pennsylvania Academy of Fine Arts.

A subject of controversy in the still Puritan America of the early 19th century, this picture illustrates the classic derivation of certain early Romantic artists who, like Vanderlyn, regarded Rome as the fountainhe ad of art.

19th CENTURY AMERICAN ART

The spirit of turbulence and revolution which marks 19th century art in most of the European countries, especially France, is notably absent from American painting. It is a curious anomaly that the period of greatest physical growth produced the purest samples of Romanticism. Over a period of forty years (1820 to 1860), census figures in America jump from two and a half million inhabitants to twenty-three million. Industrial development transformed the face of the land; wealth and power became the new ideals. From this rising materialism, the artist at first recoiled,

WASHINGTON ALLSTON.—The Deluge. New York, Metropolitan Museum.
One of the most dramatic early documents of Romanticism in America by a European-trained artist who excelled at depicting both the wild and the lyrical aspects of landscape.

taking refuge in allegories and the elevated contemplation of nature. Later he transferred this romantic outlook to the discovery of the frontier—the taming of the savage wilderness. By the second half of the century, down-to-earth curiosity produced a genre school commensurate with the bustling life of the time. This, in turn, gave way to the more international ideals of the 1880's and '90's.

One of the few artists influenced by the heroics of the Napoleonic era was John Vanderlyn, who went to Paris in 1801. An admirer of David, he was primarily a seeker after the grand historical style. His classically

THOMAS DOUGHTY.—Landscape.   New York, Metropolitan Museum.
A characteristic view of the Hudson River School by its founder who, along with his followers, for the first time presented pure landscape without moral or incident.   Doughty's work is low in tone, wide, calm and peaceful.

undraped nude, *Ariadne,* shocked Americans.   He was the first to paint Niagara Falls, one of the most remunerative subjects for the Romantic's brush.   His friendship with Washington Allston in Paris and Rome brought mutual stimulation.   Allston, class poet when at Harvard, an ardent reader of "Gothic" tales of horror in medieval trappings, also encountered in Rome Washington Irving and the English poet Coleridge, author of *Kubla Khan.* His frustrated ambition was to paint heroic figure compositions, but his *The Deluge,* showing washed-up bodies, serpents and a howling wolf against a desolation of waters, stands as the outstanding early document of American Romanticism.

Though landscape became the accepted vehicle for this school, its

Samuel F. B. Morse.—Sheldon Clark.   Yale University Art Gallery.

A typically solid, trenchant portrait by the first president of the National Academy of Design whose versatile talents eventually brought him more fame as an inventor than as an artist.

THOMAS COLE.—The Titan's Goblet.   New York, Metropolitan Museum.

Cole's imagination is of a fantastic nature which today finds an echo in Surrealism.   In addition to such pictures, he painted allegories and the first unadulterated landscapes after Doughty.

ASHER B. DURAND.—The Beeches.   New York, Metropolitan Museum.

As a leading engraver, Durand's painting has a certain meticulous stiffness. But he was highly influential in the Hudson River School, advising its young artists to work direct from nature.

JOHN FREDERICK KENSETT.—Sea and Rocky Shore.   New York,
Metropolitan Museum of Art.

*A Durand pupil, Kensett had a wider choice of subject matter and a crisp,
deliberate technique suited to his honest, accurate statement.*

FREDERICK E. CHURCH.—Heart of the Andes.   New York,
Metropolitan Museum of Art.

*Widely traveled in search of the wild and the exotic, Church represents a fusing
of the Romantic with the final expansion of the Hudson River style.*

ALBERT BIERSTADT.—Merced River, Yosemite Valley. New York,
Metropolitan Museum of Art.

*As civilization pushed west, American artists outstripped it, seeking the
Romantic in the frontier. Bierstadt was one of these, a painter of the vast and
grandiose magnified by his own imagination.*

first exponents were hard put to for a living. In the first quarter of
the 19th century artists like John Trumbull and William Dunlap painted
Niagara Falls, but as a side-line only. Samuel F. B. Morse (inventor of the
telegraph, who would have liked to be remembered as an artist rather than a
scientist) alternated his crisp portraits with precipitous views of the Alps
and idyllic stretches of the Hudson shoreline. The actual founder of the
Hudson River School was, however, Thomas Doughty who, for the first time
in American art, approached landscape as a subject sufficient in itself. His
attitude was a philosophic one, setting the note for a school which contem-
plated nature reverently as a perfect creation of God. An outdoor man who
enjoyed hunting and fishing, Doughty was technically equipped to give a

WILLIAM SIDNEY MOUNT.—Long Island Farmhouse. New York,
Metropolitan Museum of Art.

*Realism and clarity, plus a strong illustrational bent mark the work of Mount.
Already his eye for incident begins to approach the genre school of the latter
century, though there is distinction and reserve in his quiet coloring.*

competent and often poetic account of New England, the Catskills and
Pennsylvania. His "brown harmonies" had a far-reaching influence. By
his death in 1856, the cause of landscape had been well won.

The bright star of the Hudson River School (which incidentally was far
from being localized on one particular river, including as it did the Far
West, South American and Labrador) was Thomas Cole. His compelling
allegories seem like the completion of Allston's imaginings. Even straight
landscapes by Cole have an element of suspense: the sun about to break
over the eastern summits; a ragged tree ready to pitch into a foaming
torrent; a weed-grown castle which dwarfs its gesticulating admirers. Of
his allegories, *The Voyage of Life* in four parts is probably best known,

THOMAS MORAN.—The Teton Range. New York, Metropolitan Museum.
Moran, like Bierstadt, was a painter of vast western panoramas, his subjects
Yellowstone National Park, the Grand Canyon, the Rockies.

though the surreal *Titan's Goblet* and *The Architect's Dream* appeal more to the modern imagination.

Asher B. Durand was the period's leading engraver, who multiplied and made known the works of other men. His own compositions are competent, sober, like meticulous prints projected into the color dimension. His best known flight of fancy depicts his friends Thomas Cole and the poet William Cullen Bryant, both considerably overdressed for the occasion, admiring a wild Catskill stream. As the first to advocate on-the-spot painting from nature rather than studio versions made from notes, Durand is important. Epitomizing the extreme Romantic temperament is John Quidor, a bizarre depicter of hell, witchcraft and damnation in terms of Hudson Valley legends. John Kensett, greatly admired in his time, painted shadowy pools and leafy glades. His crisp way of rendering a shore-line or granite shale foreshadows Winslow Homer's watercolors.

GEORGE CATLIN.—Apache Village on Lake Ahrocum. New York,
American Museum of Natural History.

One of the numerous absorbing documents brought back from successive expedi-
tions into Indian territory by this artist. Painter, amateur ethnologist,
explorer and inveterate showman, Catlin collected souvenirs from his travels
which eventually were exhibited along with his paintings all over Europe.

The three following artists, whose dates range over a century, saw the
movement pass its apex to resolution and decline. All fulfilled their
Faustian longings for the remote and unattainable. Frederick E. Church
went furthest afield: to Latin America after volcanoes, to Labrador after
icebergs, to the West Indies. His forte was the grandiose in nature, to
which Romantics frequently attached the word "sublime." Albert Bierstadt
and Thomas Moran went west. The former's canvases, depicting the hoary
giants of the virgin forest, once brought fabulous sums. Moran painted
many of our national parks. His early interest in Turner and consequent
experiments with concentrated light-effects degenerated into somewhat
lurid sunset idylls.

HENRY INMAN.—The Young Fisherman. New York, Metropolitan Museum.
*A landscapist associated with the Hudson River School, and occasional figure
painter, Inman's work has a sentimental genre cast.*

WILLIAM M. HARNETT.—The Old Cremona.   New York,
Metropolitan Museum of Art.

*With a unique talent for verisimilitude, Harnett achieved trompe l'œil effects
which have brought him great popularity today.   On one occasion, as a result
of his rendition of a dollar bill, he was accused of counterfeiting.*

WINSLOW HOMER.—High Tide (detail).   New York, Metropolitan Museum.
A typical work by the artist who captured the very mood and feeling of the sea.

Paralleling these poetic effluvia there flowed a pithier, more literal stream
in American painting.   The realist tendency, so strong at the beginnings
of its art, ran under cover for a couple of generations, to emerge in the
work of William Sidney Mount and Henry Inman.   But where Inman's
discursiveness tends to sentimental genre, Mount is often coolly detached.
His admirable scenes of country life on Long Island foreshadow Thomas
Eakins.   They have their folksy side too—a manner that by mid-century
was growing increasingly popular.   With the enormous physical changes
that were taking place as the lusty young nation spread out to grasp its
continent, artist-reporters were needed.   The best of these include George
Caleb Bingham, whose Mississipi River scenes are classics of their kind;
the painter of Indian life, George Catlin and Eastman Johnson.   Though
trained abroad in the Düsseldorf school which was beginning to attract
new-world artists, Johnson's work is ultra-American, his local and often
charming subject-matter presented with warmth, clarity and roundness.
An isolated figure in the realist ranks is William Harnett, a painter of

THOMAS EAKINS.—William Rush Carving his Allegorical Figure of the Schuylkill River. New York, Brooklyn Museum.

This unconventional studio picture is typical of the uncompromisingly honest vision of Eakins which earned him unpopularity in his day.

meticulous still-lifes which enjoy an enormous vogue today for their trompe-l'œil and modern patterns.

By the end of the century, the two big names in realism, Winslow Homer and Thomas Eakins, come to the fore. Homer, an artist-correspondent for a newspaper in his youth, painted America's greatest seascapes; not, however, as philosophical musings about nature, but as background for the sturdy, vivid race of Maine fishermen. Hissing storms striking the granite coastline, a big catch, fog rolling into a harbor have the very smell and feel of the subject. Though favorite themes, Homer did not limit himself to these. He painted the West Indies, the backwoods and pastimes such as skating and croquet in a way that makes them infinitely alive, yet

THOMAS EAKINS.—The Actress (detail). Philadelphia Museum of Art.

An artist whose only passion was for the absolute truth of his rendition, Eakins knew how to catch his models off-guard, stripped of defences. As a portraitist, he was too honest to be popular.

WILLIAM M. CHASE.—Lady with a White Shawl. Pennsylvania Academy of the Fine Arts. *An exponent of the painting style of Munich, where he received his education, Chase's portraits are in a dark tonality which eventually, over long years of teaching, became widely imitated in American art, as was his "loaded brush" technique.*

ALEXANDER H. WYANT.—An Old Clearing.   New York,
Metropolitan Museum of Art.

*Originally a Hudson River School painter, Wyant, through his master Inness,
came in contact with the Barbizon School, and acquired from these artists a
more poetic and atmospheric interpretation.*

CHILDE HASSAM.—Washington Arch, Spring. Washington, D. C.,
Phillips Memorial Gallery.

*One of the first American Impressionists, his work differs from its French
counterpart in its harder, typically western light, an underlying sense of
realism supplanting Gallic grace.*

JAMES McNEILL WHISTLER.—Arrangement in Pink and Purple.
Cincinnati Art Museum.

The evanescent style seen most frequently in his celebrated " nocturnes " here gives a haunting quality to a figure piece. Controversial in his day, Whistler in many ways foreshadowed the moderns.

JAMES MCNEILL WHISTLER.—A Young Girl in Blue (detail). New York,
Collection Mrs. Diego Suarez.

*The influence of Oriental art, strong among painters in the 1870's, is evident
in Whistler's reticence of expression, in his occasional flat patterning.*

MARY CASSATT.—A Cup of Tea.   Boston, Museum of Fine Arts.
The painter of intimate scenes filled with a sense of living, Mary Cassatt brings a French touch to American art, paving the way for the appreciation of her master, Degas.

without niggling photographic detail.   In watercolor he developed a free technique which has been consistently imitated ever since.   Thomas Eakins was a scientific realist who, like the Dutch masters, found an operation in a hospital theatre as artistically absorbing as the delineation of a face. While studying art in his native Philadelphia, he took a physicians' course in anatomy, thereafter regarding everything he painted with a kind of surgical probity.   His portraits, often far from flattering, are unforgettable characterizations, so alive that it is easy to overlook their sober, beautiful paint quality.   Out of Eakins, overlooked in his time, grew the socalled "Ashcan" school of realists, which marked the turn into the modern age.

By the mid 19th century, America had completed the chauvinistic cycle which began with its political independence, and was again looking

ERNEST LAWSON.—High Bridge. N. Y., Whitney Museum of American Art.
Often classified as an American Impressionist, Lawson developed a personal technique which lent both glow and at the same time solidity to his broken color. His snow scenes are notable.

toward Europe as a source of superior culture. In the 1860's artists studied in Düsseldorf to learn "finish." A few years later it was the fashion to work in Munich. Here William Merritt Chase studied in 1872, returning to propound its doctrines over a long and influential teaching career. It has been said that American painting as a whole got several shades darker as the result of the Munich school, which admired fumed shadows and picturesque studio effects. However, it produced many excellent portraits, drawn freely with a heavily loaded brush to give the confident bravura effects of which Sargent was past master.

To France in 1854 went George Inness. After contact with the Barbizon painters, he brought back an illusive, atmospheric concept of landscape which eventually succeeded the Hudson River style. A fine painter, he

GEORGE CALEB BINGHAM.— Fur Traders Descending the Mississippi.
New York, Metropolitan Museum of Art.

*A successful compromise between genre and document painted with sympathy
and good humor, Bingham's pictures give a vivid account of life in the mid-
century in his native Middle West.*

evokes by mood rather than by declamation, at times achieving a Corot-like delicacy. His pupil Wyant, though not directly trained in France, combined the manner of nearly all of the Barbizon painters in a personal style.

To Europe James McNeill Whistler owes not only his style but his original recognition. In England he was influenced by the Pre-Raphaelites. In France, as a Gleyre pupil, he was subjected to the environment out of which developed Impressionism. The Japanese prints which fascinated Monet are responsible for the asymmetry of his work and the cult for understatement which culminated in those famous "arrangements," "symphonies,"

JOHN SINGER SARGENT.—Repose. Washington, D. C.,
National Gallery of Art.

and "nocturnes" that to Ruskin appeared to be "wilful imposture." Mary
Cassatt is closely associated with the Impressionist group, though actually
Degas was the forming influence on her work. It remained for Childe
Hassam and Ernest Lawson to bring to maturity the Impressionism that
a few lesser men had transplanted to this country.

After Copley and West, John Singer Sargent is the artist who won the
major laurels for American painting abroad. An international by upbringing, he painted with an effortless ease which permitted the personality of
the sitter to dominate his technical *tours de force*. His work epitomizes
the day of great, untaxed fortunes, international marriages, and a prospect
of eternal political balance. The era died hard, Sargent himself living on
into the 1920's. But it made a splendid, lingering sunset to the basically
romantic 19th century.

PIERRE BONNARD.—Summer Landscape.   Private Collection.

THE 20th CENTURY

THERE was nothing about the Exposition Universelle of 1900 to give
the informed visitor an inkling that here was as pent epoch throwing
off its last sparks.   On the contrary, everything reflected the triumph of
the style known as *art nouveau.*

A spirit of overloading animated architecture, furniture, signs.   It
reappeared in other domains of the decorative arts, recalling the curvilinear
outlines, the elegant preciosity of the Symbolists or the Nabis.

Having reached full term, officially sanctioned by this exposition, Impressionism was beginning to lay more and more stress (especially if we recall Monet and Renoir) on this pantheistic dream, this atmosphere of fluid incantation, this subtle melodic enjoyment which we will later find under another guise in the works of Debussy, Bergson and Proust.

Indeed, music, philosophy, literature no less than the plastic arts had begun to align themselves under the ægis of the "adorable arabesque," as Debussy called it. This essentially Baroque character, this apotheosis carried in itself the seeds of its own destruction.

Events began to speed up. The inception of the Salon d'Automne, in 1903, was an invitation to change. In architecture, to be sure, the movement that ran counter to *art nouveau* had already manifested itself in the last years of the old century. Under Loos in Austria, Perret in France, Berlage in Holland, Van de Velde in Belgium and later Germany, it became a violent crusade against everything over-decorated and finally against ornament in general. Comparable manifestations appear all down the line; in a few years, the break with the past had been accomplished. The new age had begun to lead men and events toward the still inscrutable future.

In its intensely agitated, tormented exterior, modern art reflects preoccupations and needs which had been in the making for the previous fifty years. By the same token, it is admittedly difficult to grasp or penetrate under its constantly varied aspects and the multiplicity of its investigations which ushered in the primitive or experimental period at the turn of the century.

At first blush, no period ever seemed more diffuse. However, over the years, certain broad lines establish themselves: the return to the origins; the precedence of instinct; the urge to geometrize or strip down; the will to power; the exaltation of collective feeling.

It is not enough merely to confirm the fact that Gauguin, from 1888 on, championed the return to the origins by trying to imbue his friends and disciples with his own admiration for rough Breton calvaries and primitive art; nor to argue which, around 1907, of Picasso, Derain and Vlaminck was the first to deify Negro sculpture; but rather to detect at every hand, well before the century's end, an impatient curiosity as to the sources of knowledge itself. Take, for instance, the magazine *l'Ymagier* of René de Gourmont and Alfred Jarry, which, before 1894, disclosed the treasures of popular imagery. Interest in folklore was also growing apace, both in the musical and the literary fields.

The trend is reiterated in the recognition of ethnology as a science. In music, it appears in themes drawn from Negro spirituals, used by Dvorak in 1894 in his Fifth Symphony, and later by Debussy in *The Golliwog's*

EDOUARD VUILLARD.—Interior.   Private Collection.

Cakewalk. In pure science, with Hannequin formulating the hypothesis of the atom, with Henri Poincaré, Langevin and Einstein, it manifests itself in the need to revise traditional notions and question the very nature of matter, time and space.

Art abounds no less with striking coincidences. Simultaneously, scholars began to busy themselves with discovering or relating the diverse aspects of the vast prehistoric world or the heretofore despised or unrecognized pre-Hellenic and pre-Roman civilizations. Excavations, explorations, inquiries and opuses multiplied. In a few decades, art history saw its field expanded ten times over. A great revision of values got under way once the Classic was no longer the ultimate standard. Primitive paintings, popular, archaic, barbaric and naïve arts were destined from this time on to hold their own in museums.

Born at the close of the nineteenth century, this movement gained in scope and energy. Physicians, mathematicians, writers, artists arrived at identical conclusions: the denial of appearances and the negation of reality. Like the primitives, they abandoned an accessible universe in favor of dizzy infinity. Similarly, artists limited themselves to fragmentary syntheses, consulting an inner world one created by intelligence alone and offering that continuity that they vainly sought elsewhere. Eventually, the overuse of the power of intelligence led them to defy it and depend only, like the primitives, on their instinctive motivations.

The precedence of instinct was destined henceforth to hold a virtually uncontested sway over the products as well as the morals of our time. Psychologists began to devote their time to it—Janet in 1883 with psychological automatism, and, after 1900, Bergson and especially Freud. Artists were the first to apprehend this. Fauvism, which appeared in 1905, and following it Expressionism, with its impetuous, lyric concatenation of form and color released from all rules, exalt the modern world's lust for life, whether joyful or sad. A similar conception—an orgy of color in décors, a barbarous and sensual dance rhythm in music—is significantly reiterated from 1909 on in the theatre of the Ballet Russe.

Musicians and writers, obeying the directives of their times, were bound to further this evolution by winning for it a wider hearing. Actively they participated in the reversal of the established order. With Stravinsky and Darius Milhaud it was primitivism and hints of European or exotic folklore, plus the total upset of the tonal system. Bursting all bounds, the musical phrase, like the sentence in literature, unfolded violently for the sole purpose of conveying the exasperated subjectivity of its creator. Honneger and Poulenc, drawn in turn toward a truculent or a meagre mode of expression, often lend it a kind of aggressive simplicity. Similarly poetry, divested of all punctuation, rediscovers with Apollinaire the fresh-

The caption under this plate should read:

HENRI MATISSE.—Decorative Panel. Private Collection.

HENRI MATISSE.—Woman with a Guitar (detail).   Private Collection.
The line is reduced to a contour and the color is localized in flat tints in order to remove from the painting all power of realistic suggestion.

ness of the direct incantation and returns to the instinctive melopoeia of Reverdy and Cendrars.

These savage forces which have invaded music, literature and painting, in which conquering dynamism and destructive fury are frantically mingled, surely find their counterparts in the screaming signs and flashing signals of our streets and still more in the development of contemporary events.

Faced with the release of these primary instincts, the artist had no choice but to transfer their vehemence to his colors and rhythms. However, intelligence rebels against such excesses. Unable to master them, it at least channels their direction. From 1908 on, the Cubists and the leading Fauves controlled themselves within the limits of a rigorous plastic convention. Thus painting found once more the basic requisites, those ancient elementary rules of expression which the more refined centuries had forgotten.

This was the moment when, as in all primitive periods, we encounter the urge to geometrize and strip down. Before long, architecture, then in turn the decorative arts, began to expound this æsthetic on a public scale both on the street (buildings, shop-fronts, signs) and in interiors.

Today, the work of art, whether picture, poem or musical composition, must be entirely divested of frills. The new concept also governed interior decoration (even though museums and salons have still not got around to banishing their gothicism in deference to the single masterpiece hung on a wall free of all ornament).

Following the admirable tenets of Cendrars, painters, poets, musicians have learned short-cuts. Unconsciously, they seek the essence of the idea, they proceed by elision, by contractions; or else they practise simultaneity and superpositioning in the manner of the early Cubists and Futurists. The external appearance of the object is correspondingly altered. To all intents, improvisation has triumphed. Still more disconcerting, the impression of confusion, disorganization, brutality is born out of the fact that the forms, brought together in an increasingly restricted area, seem to nudge one another, intersect brusquely, meet on unexpected terms. The Dadaists and Surrealists understood this and made the most of it. From their very beginnings in 1916, they were adept at unexpected encounters both in poetry and later in painting, eventually making systematic use of them. Once anarchy and the laws of chance became supreme, as was the Surrealist aim, little power was left to the intelligence.

Among the diverse personalities who put their seal on the primitivism of our century, two laid great stress on the power of the mind, thus offering the best guarantee of the future. It would, in fact, be impossible to conceive the growth of a new order not based on the will to power and the exaltation of collective feeling.

HENRI MATISSE.—The Dance. Moscow, Museum of Modern Art.

A synthesis of rhythm is the goal of Matisse in this farandole of nudes; the nervous, irregular line expresses a youthful fever of research. In the other Matisse reproduction, the sure, calm line translates the serenity which the artist has sought ever since 1906.

Lacking a common ground of thought in the social, political and religious world—that bond which relates superior minds such as doctors, mathematicians, philosophers, writers, musicians, artists—this basic principle reveals a vast unexplored universe, a universe of infinite possibility which the limitations of reality cannot circumscribe.

"The universe conceived by modern science eludes all description based on the known facts, traditional and dimensional, of the human spirit. The scholar speculates today in a reality which is beyond the range of our senses, whose mystery becomes greater as the scientific investigation penetrates the infinitesimal," observes Germain Bazin.

The vast changes which followed on this discovery provoked reversals

HENRI MATISSE.—Woman on a Couch. Private Collection.

of values of which our century is the result. Above all, they establish it as the victim of mechanization, which now was assured of unlimited development, assaulting man in his inmost being. By a curious combination, he emerges crushed and, at the same time, full of enthusiasm. In one way, he has the impression of having been deceived, humiliated, thrown back on himself, threatened by this machine to which his fate seems bound and which, at the same time, lies in wait for him. The fact is that he depends on himself to turn this machine to his uses and therefore he esteems it, in the manner of Fernand Léger. Musicians, writers, artists daily celebrate this victory over matter, over reality. The more the latter gives in to them, the more superior they feel.

Scorning all the graces of seduction, the work of art no longer tries to please. It is, on the contrary, hard, supercilious, tyrannical, favoring a tight, taut style, strict outlines, sharp contrasts, emphatic harmonies, an incisive, rigorous handwriting. Buildings, signs, shop-fronts, pictures, poems and musical compositions no longer invite the spectator discreetly; they parade before him, forcing his attention, imposing themselves brutally, aiming to address the crowd directly. In assuming this language of the demagogue, the work of art little by little becomes a part of collective experience.

GEORGES ROUAULT.—Old Clown. Hollywood,
Edward G. Robinson Collection.

In Rouault's works, the thick accentuated lines take on an almost brutal expressive force.

GEORGES ROUAULT.—The Old King. Pittsburgh, Carnegie Institute.
Rouault draws the inspiration for his colors from medieval stained glass windows, from Coptic fabrics, and Byzantine mosaics.

THE MAIN CURRENTS AND THE MASTERS
OF MODERN EUROPEAN ART

Following multiple, divergent directions and undergoing rapid evolution, modern art generally appears to the public as a series of schools or currents: Fauvism, Cubism, Futurism, Expressionism, Surrealism and so on, each one inextricably entangled with the other. To add to the confusion, artists and historians have not hesitated to baptize as an "ism" almost any system or ephemeral theory, i.e., orphism, rayonism, musicalism, etc., thus assuring themselves quick prestige in an epoque ridden by theory and with a predilection for classification.

The continuous modifications germane to the work of all artists, the complexity of inter-relationship between one group and the next, from country to country, the currents which run their course and frequently tangle, demand either simplification or arbitrary classification. Thus certain phenomena seem contradictory and well-nigh inexplicable. Whereas Paris is recognized as the international center of artistic life and attracts painters from the whole world, whereas art takes on an increasingly international character, one sees foreign countries give birth to flourishing national schools to all intents unconnected with Paris, but the outcome, under another name, of analogous investigations.

Notwithstanding, in France and elsewhere, the main currents which have come into being since the beginning of the century indicate an undeniable solidarity. They translate the multiple aspects of the war between the new forces of instinct and intelligence, channeling them, subjecting them to rules and strict discipline.

For nearly fifty years, this fight, at times explosive, at others under cover, developed with alternate results without, in the final analysis, intelligence having gained its ends. Each time that an agreement seemed about to take place, a new wave, generally set in motion by the pressure of events, put the outcome in doubt. For a time, the forces of instinct seemed to dominate art and the long-anticipated appearance of a classical equilibrium were once again postponed. The main elements in this struggle line up as follows: Fauvism, Cubism, Surrealism, Irrealism.

PIERRE-ALBERT MARQUET.—Quai de Conti Under the Rain. New York, Private Collection.

Applying to Nature the schematic tendencies of Fauvism, Marquet excels in producing the synthesis of a landscape.

KEES VAN DONGEN.—Sail in Venice.   Private Collection.

Reduced to the intersection of two arabesques and several light tones, like those of a watercolor, this picture is typical of the synthetic spirit of Fauvism.

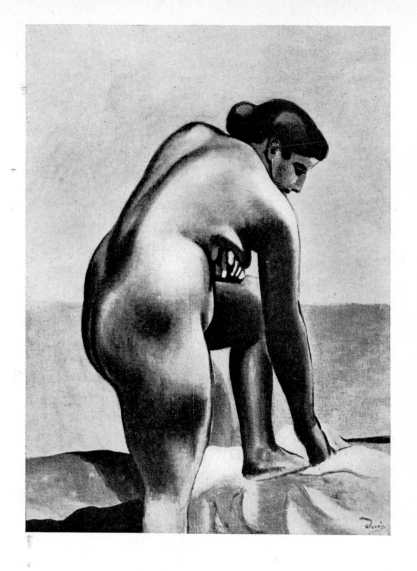

ANDRÉ DERAIN.—Study of the Nude.   Fukushima Collection.

Compared with the preceding picture, this painting shows well how Derain returned, in his maturity, to a more classical conception of art.

ANDRÉ DERAIN.—Charing Cross Bridge.　Philadelphia Museum of Art.
In 1906 and 1907 Derain tried his hand at the pure-color experiments of the
Fauves.

RAOUL DUFY.—Study of the Nude.   Paris, Private Collection.

Like Matisse, Dufy reduces line to an arabesque and color to flat tints; but he is more spontaneous and sensitive to picturesque accents.

MAURICE DE VLAMINCK.—Harbor of Marseilles.   Private Collection.

*The schematic procedures of Fauvism serve Vlaminck as a means of expressing
a dramatic sentiment of Nature.*

FAUVISM

Thanks to a scandal, Fauvism made itself known at the Salon d'Automne of 1905. The canvases in question, violently colored, harsh, their summary, jagged forms worked with a kind of barbaric robustness, their bold insouciance mingled with brutal enjoyment, violently shocked the visitors and a contingent of the critics, who complained that "a pot of paint had been thrown in the public's face."

There, in the central hall of the salon, which had been baptized for this occasion "the cage of the wild animals," were Matisse, Rouault, Marquet, Van Dongen, Derain, Vlaminck, Friesz, to mention but a few. Most of them were not unknown, having already shown at the Independents' or in galleries. But here, for the first time, they were united, giving the impression that a vast movement had just been born. They had in common not only their debut, but a passion for color and an ardent thirst for freedom.

Like Van Gogh, the Fauves wanted their color to be as intense as possible and capable of transmitting emotions directly. To this end, they chose pure tones—reds, blues, oranges which, as one of them said, "stir the ancient, sensual depths in man." To heighten these tones, they exaggerated the contrasts. With a kind of savage frenzy, they applied their color in broad strokes and large areas, frequently underscoring forms by heavy outlines, demonstrating as a whole an insatiable appetite for painting.

If a number of them, such as Vlaminck, Van Dongen, Derain, seemed didactic, it is because all of them, even the most intelligent, were impelled, by the need for sheer liberty, to behave as if they wanted to break entirely with the past and deny the earlier centuries' pictorial laws. Systematically, they neglected to finish their paintings, ignoring the scale of values, the rendition of relief, perspective, traditional modeling. In their art, as in their mode of living, they proposed to break all rules, all useless conventions. They aspired to be pure, naïve as savages or children, and dreamed of forgetting everything in order to start afresh, reconstructing with their own hands their very own universe, scaled to size and to order. Like Gauguin, they did not hesitate to turn to primitive or popular art, in which they found the apparent simplicity, the brutal vigor which they envied.

For similar reasons, most of them, faced with bourgeois conformity or the dandyism of the amateur artist, proclaimed by contrast an aggressive liberty of manners and talk. Generally dressed like laborers, habitués of the bistros and other low joints of Montmartre and elsewhere, they made a virtue of their poverty and of the fact that, to earn their living, they were at times obliged to paint buildings, sell newspapers, or make bicycle deliveries. Freely they expressed anarchist or revolutionary opinions. And soon, under their influence, which prevailed primarily between the two wars, there came into vogue a style of exaggerating the bohemian pose and, after the death of Modigliani and the chronic alcoholism of Utrillo, of promoting the legend of the "accursed painter."

Of the lot, Vlaminck, without forcing his inclination and skilfully cultivating his style, eventually came to represent to the public the archetype of the Fauve, both by his life and in his works. Even his writings did not fail to underscore this role.

At various times engaged in the most diverse professions, this artist, square, massive, athletic in build like his friend Derain, enjoyed in his early years playing the role of strong man or free man in the company of the latter. But where Derain soon became civilized, Vlaminck persevered in his mode, retiring to the country to lead the life of his Flemish ancestors, rustic and solitary to be sure, but not without comfort.

Related in their early years, the painting of these two men eventually diverged widely. Derain's painting, like that of Marquet, soon quietened down and, while remaining vigorously assertive, grew more refined, more knowing. Vlaminck's, on the contrary, evolved toward a more impulsive and flashing style. Retaining his original impetus, augmenting it even, Vlaminck, like Van Dongen and Friesz (though less subtly, and with more abandon and violence than the latter) brushes his canvases with generous ardor in a flowing style and heavy impasto. Following the example of all the other Fauves except Matisse, he little by little began to abandon his pure palette, his over-violent contrasts for more muted harmonies which he darkened with earth tones—blues and blacks—scored with hasty slashes of white or color which give his skies a stormy look and lend an oppressive heaviness even to the atmosphere of his interiors.

This same procedure was taken over in turn, with brio and emphasis, by the generation of Dunoyer de Segonzac and his friends.

However, nourished by Fauvism itself, another trend began to make itself felt about 1907-1908. Here Matisse was the guiding force and for this occasion registered a veritable act of faith. Oldest member of a movement whose main animator and instigator he had been, he proposed to stem this tide of instinctive expression with some strictness, some restraint.

The memory of Cézanne and his rigorous constructions is immediately called to mind. And indeed, for several years, nearly all of the Fauves were haunted by his obsessions, to a point where Braque, newcomer to the group, dedicated himself exclusively to Cézanne's theory and soon founded Cubism. The others, thanks to the war, were not long in falling back into their old habits, abandoning themselves gratefully to the demands of their temperaments.

Matisse remained more or less solitary in pursuing the difficult path upon

OTHON FRIESZ.—View of the Port at Toulon.   Private Collection.
In his best works Friesz is adept at retaining in his line and color all the spontaneity of a sketch.

which he had embarked. Possessed of a sound pictorial technique, gifted with rare intelligence, intuitive, methodical, he applied himself to analyzing his instinct in order to exert over it control and the power of choice. His job was to rediscover emotion—which, in all its purety and freshness, came as something of a shock.

Color for him retained all its importance and brilliance. It is spread boldly in big, vigorous areas which balance one another and establish their own equilibrium. Merely by contrast, they suggest space. In spite of their intensity, they are seductive, they radiate, thanks to the knowing audacity of their chords, the decorative suppleness of the arabesques they enclose. For this painter, far removed from the emotional, flamboyant fantasies of his colleagues, sought the art of stability, quietude and charm. He attained it through utmost simplicity, harmony of line and inter-relationship of color from which emanate a broad sense of calm.

It was this kind of mastery, re-stated without deviation until the present day, which, both in France and abroad, had widespread repercussions, assuring Matisse the premier place among contemporary artists over the last forty years. This reputation is equalled only by Bonnard who, refusing to subscribe to the increasingly facile and affected manner of the other Nabis, attained a no less living expression of serenity and happiness through nothing more than his singing color. With this color, he combined a kind of spontaneous humor and a delicate sensitivity which lends his vision, especially in sketches, a deft subtlety, an element of poetic surprise. Painted by fragmentary touches but fused into large color areas, his works, especially the late Mediterranean landscapes painted just before his death, have a vibrant intensity, a quality of sunshine which gives them true glow. Bonnard, like Matisse who has lived there since 1917, had settled on the Côte d'Azur because of its mild climate and its atmosphere of amiable serenity.

Dufy, by his fresh imagination and joyful exuberance, deserves to take his place alongside of these two artists. Of the harshness and stiffness of the other Fauves, he retained nothing. As easily as a bird sings, he expresses himself on his canvas with a facility and a free outpouring of ideas not inferior to Matisse, the reality of the picture being, even more than with the latter, reduced to a few graphic strokes scattered in lively stenography according to the inspiration of the painter.

THE INSTINCTIVE PAINTERS

During the period when Fauvism and, shortly after, Cubism began to make themselves felt, another trend was grafted onto the current of art.

HENRI ROUSSEAU, called THE DOUANIER.—The Woman with the Serpent
(detail).   Paris, Musée du Louvre.

*Rousseau's large compositions are exotic evocations and works of imagination,
with a profound poetry that makes one think of the works painted by Gauguin
at Tahiti.*

HENRI ROUSSEAU, called THE DOUANIER.—The Cart of Father Juniet.
Paris, Private Collection.

*The naivety with which Rousseau paints Nature leads him to schematic qualities
that are related to those of Fauvism.*

It developed rapidly in these same Montmartre environments which, before
the first World War, had played so important a role.

Although the artists of the Butte, the poets (among them in particular
Guillaume Apollinaire) and finally amateurs made much of the neglected
genius of the Douanier Rousseau and the early works of Utrillo, it was
not until after the war that the cult made headway and that this type of

MAURICE UTRILLO.—The House of Berlioz (detail). Private Collection.

Utrillo was the first to introduce into landscape painting the desolation of the suburbs with their shabby narrow streets, and the sadness of the outlying parts of town with their ageless houses void of style.

painting as a whole became accredited. Today, snobbism has succeeded in giving it more importance than is its due.

One should not, however, regard the Douanier Rousseau as purely naïve. He has, of course, simplicity of heart, humility in front of nature as a work of art, the probity of the professional and a sense of craftsmanship. He respected all the conventions, both as to outer style and interpretation, and wished only to imitate Meissonnier or Bouguereau at the very time when the latter had fallen from favor. Nevertheless, this autodidactic customs officer who painted out of instinct and pure passion for paint, succeeded by unflagging work from the year 1884 on in acquiring an excellent technique. In addition, he had an astonishing gift for color and his confiding, almost proud ingenuousness became for him a source of dreams and poetry. Without even realizing what he was doing, he clumsily, patiently imagined a world made to order which to-day moves us by its touching frankness.

Nor is Utrillo quite as naïve as people like to imagine. Although he formed his style independently, his mother Suzanne Valadon stood at his side, as did his step-father and old friend, Alfred Utter. Both gave him useful advice. Utrillo was an invalid, hyper-nervous, a born neurasthenic upon whom alcoholism preyed, ultimately bringing physical breakdown. To him, painting was an escape and a means of redemption. In his instinctive rapture, he confided to it his distress and his hopes. Regardless of subject, he had acquired since 1909 the habit of working from postcards. In his soul there was simplicity. Utrillo reveals himself to us discreetly, with sincerity, never forcing his style. Through the medium of dilapidated walls, sordid back streets, church spires launched at the sky, he eternally relives (although more superficially in the last twenty years) the memories of his youth on the Butte with its moments of mystical, adolescent wonder.

After the death of Rousseau, stimulated by the sudden success which finally, by the end of the last war, greeeted the paintings of Utrillo, naïveté became elevated to the front rank as a new art form. Promptly, there developed a copious school of unsophisticated painters whose number has been constantly added to since, but of whose art little deserves to be remembered. With them arose a school of instinctive painting of undeniable, eloquent charm, freshness and a kind of state of grace all too rare in our time. But ask no more from them. These artists cannot exceed the bounds of their narrow universe.

FRENCH EXPRESSIONISM

Associated for better or worse with Fauvism, an early exponent of the teachings of Gustave Moreau and officially his inheritor, Rouault, intro-

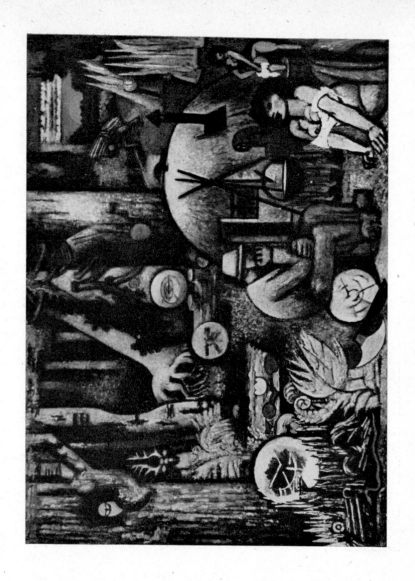

Marcel Gromaire.—The Wood.   Paris, Museum of Modern Art.
Gromaire draws his inspiration from scenes of real life, but he imposes on his figures a geometric simplification which he borrows from the Cubists.

EDOUARD GOERG.—The Big-Game Hunter. Private Collection.

It is with an intention toward Expressionism that the artist voluntarily deforms the anatomy of these nude figures.

ANDRÉ DUNOYER DE SEGONZAC.—Moret Lock (detail).   Paris, Georges Lévy Collection.—*By means of his thick impasto, Segonzac gives an earthly solidity to the landscapes he paints.*

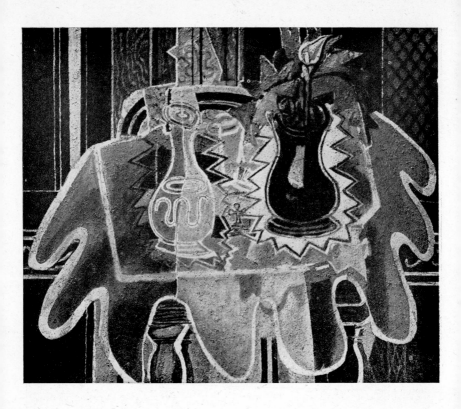

GEORGES BRAQUE.—Still-Life.   Private Collection.

Braque demands that his objects lend themselves to the rhythms and harmonies which are for him the goal of painting.   However, he is never intolerant in this respect, and sometimes even accepts objects with all the simplicity of their natural appearance.

duced into painting an unfamiliar violence and eloquent distortion.   The solution of formal problems (which he by no means neglected) was secondary with him to expressing his revolt in human terms.   Fulminating and scolding, he overwhelmed society with his irony erecting against it a case comparable to Daumier's in the guise of portraits which are near-caricatures. Prostitutes, judges, clowns and circus folk he painted in a series of con-

CHAIM SOUTINE.—Woman with Arms Folded.   Private Collection.

CHAIM SOUTINE.—The Pastry Cook at Cagnes.   Paul Guillaume Collection.

The broken and almost grimacing line, as well as the tones of clotted blood and livid white, express the violence of a disenchanted soul.

JULIUS PASCIN.—Salome. Paris, Petit Palais.
It is in a melancholy mood that the Roumanian Pascin expresses his despair.

MARC CHAGALL.—Composition.   Private Collection.

Chagall's art is poetic imagery which finds its source in the sentimental and fantastic folklore of the Slavic Jewish environment where the artist spent his youth.

AMEDEO MODIGLIANI.—Reclining Nude.   Paul Guillaume Collection.

By the beauty of their sharp arabesque which recalls that of the Tuscan painters of the Middle Ages and Renaissance, Modigliani's figures attain a high quality of style.

ventionalized but eternal heads.   At times, driving his irony home, he depicted massacres whose purpose it was to plead the cause of human dignity. His religious belief, translated in no less violent terms, is of an impressive grandeur although, before it was accepted, it scandalized Catholic circles for years.   This late recognition has been aided by Rouault's subsequent evolution toward a quieter art form.

Rouault's painting springs forth like a cry from the depths of the soul, like a call of anguish.   His color, vitrified like enamel, flares in his purples, and deep blues, is bezeled like mediaeval stained-glass windows between heavy black borders which suggest cruel torments.

GEORGES BRAQUE.—Still-Life with Flowers.   Private Collection.

But this suggestive form, this visionary accent, this profound pathos no longer belongs to Fauvism. Another mode had been born, as yet nameless. Withdrawn into the solitude of his labors, Rouault never proposed to head a school. Nevertheless, increasing response not only from France, but even more from foreign countries soon consolidated his echo. Since then, Expressionism, as so called in Rouault's preferred northern countries, has developed enormously thanks to the tragic turn of world events.

Well before the end of the first World War, the underlying nostalgia of the foreign artists living in France made them likely material for a new art movement. Thus the generation which succeeded the Fauves came to swell the ranks of modern art. Of the combatants, certain were missing, others returned imbittered by four years of suffering and anxiety, some were wounded. The false face of the post-war era indignated them. Promptly, they resorted to its language. Take the work of Gromaire. His rough-hewn figures—soldier or peasant—he plants uncompromisingly, their majestic bulk filling every inch of the canvas with mute reproach. Fortunately, his innate sensuality comes through in his color, mitigating his over-severe geometric distortions. Of this genre too is Goerg, who rides his theme still harder, underscoring without benefit of make-up, with cruel, perspicacious humor, the new society's weaknesses. His flower-women are venomous and perverse until the play of his jeweled color makes them seem to smile.

Violent as were at one time its denunciations, French Expressionism retained throughout its contacts with foreign movements a sense of measure, restraint and decency. Rather than abandon itself to imprecation and useless frenzy, it preferred to deepen its experience by turning inward for release.

THE SCHOOL OF PARIS

To demand this measure of the foreign artists who composed what came to be known as the School of Paris would have been to deny them their very nature. By atavism and, no doubt, as a result of the tragic lives many of them had led, a dull anguish throttles them, a sense of insecurity torments them. Throughout their work they express this, at times with a tragic vehemence, like Modigliani and Soutine, at others in a mood of poetic nostalgia, like Pascin and Chagall. With all of them, technique and color even more than subject matter betray a latent sadness, an inborn intellectual pessimism.

Fate was certainly least kind to Modigliani. Yet with all his indulgence of alcohol and the life of bohemianism which brought him unsavory

PABLO PICASSO.—Three Musicians.   Paul Rosenberg Collection.
*By this grouping of forms which overlap each other, the artist seeks to attain
a harmony of all the elements in his unified painted surface.*

publicity, he created in a mere ten years a remarkable life-work cut short by his death in 1920. His studies of attenuated nudes arranged in sensual arabesques recall his Italian inheritance and, even more, his beginnings, first as draftsman, then as sculptor. Beneath their stylized distortions, their look of meager distinction and the ultra-refinement of line and harmony, one senses the artist's insistent, latent despair. With Soutine, this despair is given free play and unleashes itself at random. The total picture, including the forms themselves, seems carried away in a torrent of boiling lava. Soutine's chaotic landscapes, his still-lifes which almost run blood, his convulsed faces suggest an appalling Dance of Death, counteracted, however, by the explosive color which, in the last years of his life to some extent relieved the tension of his work.

An eternal wanderer his wordly success notwithstanding, Pascin sublimated this tragic sense until the day when he yielded to long-contemplated suicide. His painting, with its nervous line, its veiled, acid harmonies, reiterates a parallel disenchantment and bitter laughter.

Alone Chagall, found providential shelter in dreams—a confused, checkered dream pierced by lightning color, compound of childhood memories, the millenial legends of Russia and the mystic aspirations of his race. When he paints a picture, Chagall hurls himself upon his canvas as if to rid himself of a grievous illness which will not leave him in peace.

CUBISM

Paralleling Matisse, who voluntarily put the brake on the extremes of Fauvism and imposed upon its instinctive forms of release strict rules and plastic order, other contemporary artists prepared to carry on this common urge toward precision.

Braque, the product of Fauvism, and Picasso, who had dabbled in a certain kind of Expressionism, discovered one another around 1907-1908. Both were in a similar state of flux, both in search of true discipline. One by one, Léger, Gris, Delaunay, Villon and many others joined them. Cubism was born. It was necessary however, to wait several years before it made a public appearance, justified its existence by some sort of manifesto and officially accepted its name.

Braque was no more thirsty of intellectualism and logic than were Picasso and Léger. Dogmatic all three, they still were less so than Matisse. To their society gravitated poets, litterateurs, critics, artists who proposed, during the course of their friendly reunions at the Bateau-Lavoir (where, incidentally, most of them lived) or in the cafés of the Butte, to develop

PABLO PICASSO.—Head of a Woman (detail).
Paris, André Lefèvre Collection.

In his first attempts at Cubism, Picasso took his inspiration from the geometrical forms of primitive Negro masks.

PABLO PICASSO.—Figure. Private Collection.

After about 1934, Picasso made use of the Cubist methods of fragmentation to create monstrous forms which express the outburst of cruelty to which the world was then giving vent.

PABLO PICASSO.—Girl with Basket of Flowers (detail). Gertrude Stein Collection.

This painting of the Rose Period, which follows immediately after the Blue Period, exhibits that expression of distress and melancholy which characterizes all Picasso's work before the discovery of cubism.

through their works new pictorial laws and erect systems for their application.

In actual fact, they worked without formula or method (their constant evolution proves this) and without predictable results, even though they often appeared to function concertedly, ending up with identical conclusions. Each followed his bent, obeying impulses which developed spontaneously, each was progressively enriched by experience and served like Braque and Léger, by infallible craftsmanship, in others, like Picasso, by an extraordinarily lively temperament.

The revolutionary action undertaken by Fauvism against the multiple conventions adopted since the Renaissance made victorious headway. Following the example of color, form in turn was relieved of direct relationship with reality and even of the notion of resembling nature. The artist was free to fragment it, to curtail it, to associate it at random or to use it as a simple hieroglyph. For now he was beginning to construct a universe precisely fitted to his needs.

This tour de force was achieved by intelligence dissimulated behind instinct, following it closely step by step, making use of its intensity of feeling but shaping it to its severe regime and, above all, eliminating elements derogatory to its power such as anecdotal reporting, easy sensuality of pigment or the common sentimental prejudice associated with familiar objects, such as the human figure.

In its first phase, called Analytic Cubism, which was halted by the first World War, the artists involved devoted themselves to minutious experiments within the pictorial dimension of painting. Banning effects of brushwork, decorative arabesques and color—the latter restricted to dull, austere tones in the grey-to-earth scale—they undertook to isolate basic structural rhythms. Like primitives, they were compelled to a rigorous simplification of form and volume, i.e., reduction to simple geometric and units of the circle, the sphere, the triangle, the cone, etc., all of these stylized rendered semi-transparent like prismatic facets.

To extend this feeling of rhythm throughout the canvas, they multiplied the angles of vision as if each object were being seen simultaneously from several points of view—from below, above, right or left. Reality, thus broken down, dissociated, suggested by fragment, eventually disappeared in certain pictures in favor of a pure abstract plan, its presence only occasionally recalled by *collage* or painstaking imitation of printers' type samples.

This revolutionary creative effort, marked by works of a sober but transcendent grandeur, did not survive the war even among those artists who, like Picasso and Gris, took no part in the struggle. A general spirit of consentment, an abuse of the basic system appeared at the beginning of

The objects are repeatedly fragmented and flattened out on the plane of the canvas; thus all conventional expression of space and suggestion of realism are lost.

FERNAND LEGER.—The Railway Station.   Balay and Carré Collection.
The sharpness of the forms, the simplicity of the colors, and the straightness of the lines and planes are all borrowed from the aesthetics of the machine.

the second phase, which is called "Synthetic Cubism," despite the fact that it was several years before it qualified for this name.   With almost all of its exponents, it had been a means of sloughing off a perhaps over-strict discipline as well as a return to lyricism, color, appearance and the human form.

The best of them, though true to their respective temperaments, continued

ROBERT DELAUNAY.—The Eiffel Tower.   Private Collection.

*In his numerous paintings of the Eiffel Tower, Delaunay has tried to express
the dynamic quality of the modern world.*

to enrich their rythms, rendering them more complex thanks to a close-knit design and color scheme, increasing dynamism and impetus.

With Braque, this continuity is manifested at its best. It justifies the position which he held for years alongside Matisse and Picasso as one of the leaders of modern art. Sober and measured, amiable but reserved, he reveals himself in his works and in his life of unostentatious, voluntary retirement. Beneath his fortunate boldness one senses a calm human being, sure of his form, subscribing without stint to the enjoyment of creating. Seen to-day in perspective, his interiors and still-lifes renew the miracle of Chardin in their thoughtful atmosphere, their tender, almost religious enjoyment. The majestic ordering of their elements, their harmonious marriage of greens and browns, of subtly-orchestrated beiges and blacks, their almost seductive quality of reserve emanate a sense of quietude and encompassing musicality. His abbreviated but none the less vigorously-defined forms link together like a vivid, unexpected sequence in a ballet. Transposed, simplified, dissociated, reality is transfigured in Braque's world, and becomes increasingly luxuriant, increasingly, quietly expressive.

Despite appearances, Picasso, for all his turn-abouts and his so-called Ingres or Classical period, his fluttering between Expressionist distortion and abstract stylization, shows corresponding consistency. Object of the most vicious insults, abusively praised, disproportionately admired, surrounded by a coterie of disciples, leading a life of bohemian luxury, he conspired for years to present himself in the role of a star. Fond of paradoxes, frolics and jokes, he never in any way attempted to dispel the equivocal misunderstandings which consistently have attached to his personality and name. His superior detachment, his spirit of independence amounting to revolt (both typically Spanish) are illustrated in his life no less than in his creations and in large measure justify them.

In his works, Picasso shows himself to us exactly as he is. Of a brilliant intelligence and mobile temperament, given to extremes, tormented, never satisfied, he is an impassioned being who proclaims his own personal drama and echoes with corresponding intensity the tragedy of our time, as is manifest in his celebrated decoration, *Guernica*, painted to commemorate the Spanish war. For Picasso is profoundly Spanish to the point of being devoured by sensuality and at the same time haunted by death. From this results a kind of morbid frenzy, an urge to cruelty, an insatiable desire which he controls only with difficulty. At any moment, his self-imposed discipline, the architecture with which he builds his canvas might tremble and burst apart under the pressure of his savage, impetuous rhythms.

Prodigious creator of forms whose elements he draws from all sides, Picasso likes to run their gamut before organizing them plastically into a

ROGER DE LA FRESNAYE.—The Gunners.   Paris, Galerie Pierre Collection.

Less abstract than Braque and Picasso, La Fresnaye retains a noticeable
attachment to the forms of reality and he imposes upon them a geometric
stylization which recalls that of Paolo Uccello.

kind of living triangulation.   If his work has proved weighty in deciding
the future of modern art, it is perhaps because of this emotional instability,
these overweening fears strangely mingled with sarcastic humor, this
frantic character in which our time will eventually recognize its own portrait with horror, while appreciating Picasso's intercession in its behalf.

Among the innumerable artists who were drawn into his wake, few could resist the temptation of imitating him, even though lacking his feverish passion both for creation and arbitrary destruction. Juan Gris, however, is one of the exceptions, perhaps because, being also Spanish, he shrinks from redundant statement, perhaps because of his short-life span. The work which he has left has a haughty self-confidence, a severe, concentrated look and the well-considered boldness of the early, so-called "Analytic" Cubism.

On the other hand, many of the artists who had joined the movement at the time of its formation or shortly after, such as Léger, Delaunay, Villon, soon liberated themselves of their own accord from the tyrannical and annihilating rule of Picasso and, to a lesser degree, of Braque. It was their task to give Cubism a new orientation which we can recognize today as being of equal importance at the time and perhaps even more fruitful. Less known as a result of fashion or snobbism, living more apart from the world, wielding less authority, they nevertheless had a determining influence, the first-mentioned on the decorative arts of the past quarter-century, the other two on the development of abstract or non-representational art forms.

Of a vigorous nature, Léger has the quiet assurance of certain strong personalities who refuse to hamper their lives with complications and remain solidly in contact with reality. Simplifying his problems, reducing his forms to a bare essential—a kind of object-type—he extracts a powerful, elementary synthesis which is a true popular language, and proceeds to carpenter it patiently. Greatly impressed by modern dynamism, enthusiastic at the triumph of the machine, he transforms a world of pistons and gears into a living diagram of strict outlines and vigorous, increasingly brilliant color areas. Beginning with man and lately extending even to nature, the whole universe becomes mechanized, eventually carried away by the heavy rhythms of the machine.

Attempting primarily to translate a kind of vibration of volumes in space, Delaunay, who was equally obsessed by the theory of motion, soon sacrificed everything to this idea, even appearance (he was the first Cubist to do this, along with Kupka and Villon). He soon hit upon a unique system of alternating colored circles. Thanks to simultaneous interplay of contrasts, these multicolored discs, harmoniously combined, build up an impression of rapidity and of circular motion, becoming in themselves a means of lyric expression. The decorative applications of Delaunay's formula were amply exploited in the post-war period.

Despite the intellectual prestige which, from the first, Villon enjoyed among the friends who voluntarily grouped themselves around him, he has only recently been promoted to the front rank as a result of his influence

ANDRÉ LHOTE.—Landscape (detail).   In the Artist's Collection.
André Lhote has attempted to readapt to reality the abstraction of the Cubists.

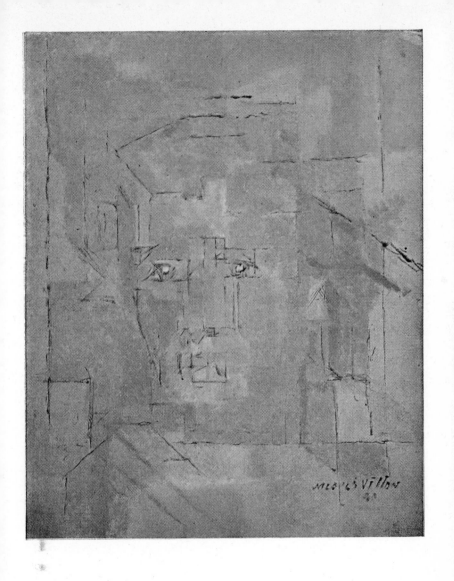

JACQUES VILLON.—Portrait of Anne D... Private Collection.
More than all the other Cubists, Villon strove toward expression by means of color.

MAX ERNST.—Night on the Rhine. Private Collection.

Thanks to artificial elements, mingled with others which he borrows from reality, Max Ernst invents an imaginary universe whose presence strikes us with hallucinating force.

on younger-generation artists and a return of public interest. Minutious construction, sharp, compact drawing, an exact sense of values plus exhaustive experiment in a language of abbreviation all contribute constructively, making of each canvas a veritable symphony of color, creating a universe which, if scarcely related to reality, is rich in the luxuriant atmosphere of poetry and expression.

This more and more general recourse to intelligence, this growing arbitrariness based on an intellectual re-ordering might seriously have endangered Cubism by threatening to stifle the gifts of nature and by undermining creative effort had not a sensitive, militant intelligence counteracted these pernicious symptoms. La Fresnaye and Lhote, co-exhibitors in the first group-showings of the movement, became the champions of this new manner.

Only the tragic circumstances of La Fresnaye's life—tuberculosis contracted during the war which led to his death—justify his original support of Cubism's illusory doctrine and his sudden, subsequent reaction in favor of an unfortunate type of mannerism. At the same time, his earlier attitude had already proved (as with several of his contemporaries) that he was superior to the general run of conformists. Burning behind him the bridges of analytical experiment, he proposed to create an immediate, expressive synthesis and a return to life in contrast to the other Cubists who banded together in painting still-life. Better armed than most of them in his cultivation, education and special gifts, he soon came into full possession of his means. His intellectuality, superior refinement and monumental feeling enabled him to endow a severely thought-out, well-defined composition with plasticity and brave color and rhythm. Such a deliberate, basic agreement of means opened wide prospects to his art which unhappily remains unfulfilled.

SURREALISM

The excesses of Cubist discipline, the ponderous, constant recourse to intelligence, the straining after a premeditated plan of construction, the submission to an omnipotent rule and sacrifice of every last creative spark were bound to induce reaction. In the northern countries and even in parts of France, Expressionism was already regaining its sway.

The Dada movement, which was born in Switzerland in 1916, appeared as a revolt, a desperate protest of the individual, an assertion of the will to live in the face of social obligation. Faced with the unprecedented breakdown of reason, the horrible betrayal of confidence and human hopes, the only outlet was absurdity, the void, the complete negation of the rational world. Soon groups were formed, made up primarily of the literary talents of France, Germany and even the United States. They engaged in a frantic effort to destroy, by means of ridicule and scandalous publicity, all accepted standards and at the same time to undermine the prestige of reason.

Before they had scattered over the world, these refractory elements met in Paris for a few years. The poet André Breton proposed to give their

ANDRE MASSON.—Combat.   Private Collection.

The painting of André Masson is permeated by a shudder of violence;
"struggle" is the leitmotiv of his art.

subversive enterprise a less negative character and explore to the full this
defensive reaction of instinct.   Surrealism, which he founded in 1924 and
still rules undisputed, became an unprecedented glorification of the instinctive forces.   It was defined by him in his first and successive manifestos

as: "Psychic automatism by means of which we propose to define . . . . the true function of thought, dictated in the absence of all control of reason and situated beyond æsthetic or moral preoccupations." Further the aims of Surrealism were "to give back its original freshness to the thinking process" and to "try to perceive more and more clearly what resides, unknown to the individual, within the depths of his mind."

The following year, André Breton presented his first group show of Surrealist artists. In it figured Masson, Miro, Klee, Max Ernst and Chirico, to be later joined by Dali and others.

When it comes to the immediate transcription of consciousness, two methods offer themselves to the Surrealists: to explore the domain of the irrational; and to liberate everything stifled, hardened by habit and conformism, thus carrying the effort into the realm of psychological investigation. Whether making use of automatic writing, which merely means permitting the creative instinct to express itself freely in the face of reality, whether consulting dreams with all their obsessions, their sexual frustrations, their unlikely sequences, their mysterious associations, here was a means of discovering those buried impulses which elude reason but which Freud, in his recent books, has proved to be behind even the smallest human act.

In what seems almost a linear debauch, in interlacing, sensuous curves feverishly scattered over the canvas, Masson seems to deliver himself of a deep sense of tragedy frequently colored by eroticism. His cursive, hasty writing quivers with an intense, innate life, the canvases are animated by a prodigious seething of forms and personages. Withal, this eruption remains the expression of a painter in possession of his best talents, master of the lyricism to which he gives such intelligent rein.

No less lucid and impulsive in his mustering of poetic images, Miro brings to them an elegant fantasy which dissembles the profound seriousness of the true Spaniard. The strange, heterogeneous symbols with which he sows his empty spaces, their sonorous colors suggest totemic incantations and convey genuine magic power.

Recoiling from anything even indirectly related to the physical world, Klee proceeds by roundabout allusion, even by contradiction. His *graffiti*, his color spots intermingled with a rare delicacy, his fragile rubbings burgeoning into intangible form have the charm of suggestion, gradually drawing the observer under their spell.

Related to the latter in his methods, Max Ernst is more brutal and peremptory. His paintings and, above all, his astonishing *collages* bespeak a taste for the fantastic and bizarre. Chance alone rules the encounters of fashion drawings, old anatomical charts, pages from obsolete natural history books, all of them cut up, juxtaposed at random, giving an impression

SALVADOR DALI.—Plate wite Telephone.   Private Collection.

*The presence of these objects, painted with uncanny realism, assumes a
disquieting character suggestive of hidden mystery.*

which is somehow evil, sacrilegious, even painful.   Such experiments have
been systematically developed by Dali who, with maximum technical ability,
plus pretentious cynicism, describes his erotic delirium and the obsessions
peculiar to his own make-up.

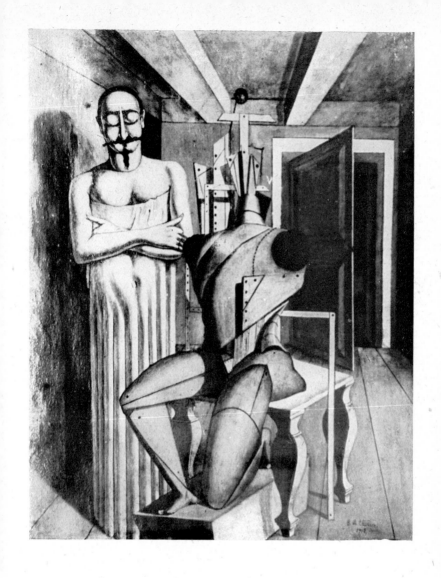

GIORGIO DE CHIRICO.—Homage to Cavour. Private Collection.

Chirico's manikins are like a ridiculous symbol of Humanism and a satire on Academism.

JOAN MIRO.—Dutch Interior. Paris, Galerie Pierre Collection.
*The early works of the Spaniard Miro evoke the magic signs of the art of Negro
or Polynesian tribes.*

JOAN MIRO.—The Farmer's Wife (detail). New York,
Pierre Matisse Collection.

During his pre-war Surrealist period (which he later reneged and which antedates, both in Italy and elsewhere, the official formation of the movement) Chirico also claimed the imaginary world, introducing into his canvases an eccentric clutter of figures, objects and other diverse elements symbolically conceived, such as old picture postcards or forgotten problems of geometry, set within a frame. This startling displacement produces a sensation of disquieting mystery.

Likewise in France Jean Lurçat, without ever having actually belonged to the Surrealist group, follows a parallel course and maintains in his canvases an intensely poetic and often strange atmosphere. But it is chiefly in tapestry that he fully realises his talent, after having spent many years studying thoroughly the various aspects of that technique. Overthrowing all the prejudice and so-called tradition developed during the last four centuries, he returns to the strict simplicity of the Middle Ages and to the discipline of limited tones. Thus he inspires a rebirth of French tapestry which has continued to flower magnificently since 1938.

Thanks to this aberration, this recurrent agony of Surrealism, as well as to the powerful, poetic evocation of its best works, the movement triumphed, recruiting in France and before long abroad adherents among the younger artists who were victims of a despair brought on by the financial crises and the new rumblings of war.

CONTEMPORARY IRREALISM

Scattered by the conflict of 1914-1918, shaken by the feverish rumors of the post-war period, yielding to an atmosphere of indifference, the new-generation painters appeared slowly. As a result, during nearly the entire period between the two wars, we find fluctuation of purpose and dispersal into rival camps. No movement succeeded in establishing itself with assurance except Surrealism and even it was not free of coterie rivalries and easy facility.

Heading a group which avoided taking any extreme stand, Brianchon and Legueult commenced their careers in the wake of Matisse and the Nabis. Their only principle was to abandon themselves to their feelings, this, however, with moderation and tact. Reality is interpreted by them as a pleasant but superficial play of tones whose vibrations their pictures describe.

At the same time, Desnoyer (whose qualities have only recently been recognized), working in virtual isolation, managed to extract more meaning from his art. Passionately absorbed by color as well as construction, he harmonizes the two in a powerful, rhythmic idiom which mirrors every

RAYMOND LEGUEULT.—The Rose. Private Collection.

Legueult belongs to the generation which, after 1930, tried to reconcile Modern Art with actual appearances.

Maurice Brianchon.—Masquerade. Private Collection.

It is a sort of a "Matisse in the flesh" that Brianchon tries to create; his odalisques do not belong to the abstract world of painting, nor do they let one forget the studio model who posed for them.

aspect of the spectacle of life.   An eloquent representative of Cubism and Fauvism, he is at the same time one of the pioneers of the rising style of Irrealism.   This can be described as a process by which the artist concentrates all his subjective energies on recreating a more complete, intenser universe thanks to the fact that he is less distracted by formal preoccupations, thus permitting instinct to refind its conquering vitality, its joyful, healthy ardor of expression.   This robust æsthetic health, this boisterous good nature is supplanted in the case of Borès and Beaudin

MAURICE ESTEVE.—Shed in Auvergne.   Private Collection.

*Esteve belongs to the recent group of Neo-Cubists who have sought a renovation
of abstract art through color.*

(who play a similar role in the contemporary art picture) by a more dolorous
temperament.

Already public interest was turning in another direction.   The economic
crisis ushered in by the year 1930 took special effect in the realm of the arts.
Subsequent social and international upheavals further added to the
confusion.

EDOUARD PIGNON.—Ostend. Private Collection.

*Pignon's most recent works show how, by patient elaboration, the artist draws
a decorative rhythm from a scene taken from nature.*

ALFRED MANESSIER.—The Engulfed Cathedral. Private Collection.

*Just as the Cubists of 1910 sought an interplay of forms, Manessier delights
in an interplay of colors which lose all attachment to reality.*

ANDRÉ MARCHAND.—The Sister. Paris, Musée d'Art Moderne.
Marchand's cutting line and irregular forms reveal a dramatic awareness which found an excellent occasion to display itself in the war.

During this period, however, a new generation arose, orientated itself as a group and bravely set out to apply the lessons learned and the victories won by the "old masters" of modern art.

Among talents which began to emerge around 1935, André Marchand and Gruber came to the forefront. Both show a certain indebtedness to the tragic manner of the Surrealists, although this trait is also an instinctive reaction to violence which, one suspects, is kept under control by intelligent volition. As the years advance, this undertone of suffering, this atmosphere of anxious waiting grew while events ran their course. In his dry, cutting strokes, Gruber becomes increasingly prone to this kind of dramatic expression.

The war, succeeded by painful upheavals in France, induced a spontaneous remustering of force among the younger painters. Beginning with the year 1941, there is evidence of unexpected meetings of minds, of unforeseen accord in experiment. Irrealism, in which Marchand, Pignon, Estève and Manessier were destined to become the leading figures, eventually justified its existence.

A triumphant impetus permeates the style of these artists, proclaims it, enriches their palettes, leads them to renew the bonds with Fauvism and Cubism in order to give them a more direct, human application. Once again, painting becomes a powerful means of expression, developing itself in broad, assertive designs, highly-colored areas and strong contrasts.

It is a proud, sturdy language, shorn of all anecdote, pre-eminently synthetic and pictorial ; thanks to transpositions, however, which subtle and daring though they frequently are, never cease, in their interplay, to be immediate and unsystematic, its appearance is often hard to grasp.

This chromatic explosion gradually fined down in the work of most of its exponents, taking on nuances, enriching greys and blacks as rhythms become more compelling and at the same time more subtle. With Marchand, preoccupation with the object and above all with light induces him to retain form at least in part. Pignon, gifted with an exceptionally vigorous temperament, like a number of his colleagues, prefers to give free rein to lyricism. Finally, with others including Estève and in particular Manessier who had already achieved an astonishing degree of mastery, the urge to strip down to the very bones and achieve greater spirituality leads these artists to non-representational art—that is, to retain out of their expression only the purest formal symbols, turning their picture into a simple area of intense color. The grandiose ordering, the noble seriousness of the work of almost all of these artists seems to presage a result comparable to the heroic efforts of Cubism. In a trend which vainly attempts to underwrite a belated rebirth of abstraction, intelligence again appears about to triumph. Whether it will succeed is the next question.

FRANÇOIS DESNOYER.—Nude.   Private Collection.

JEAN LURÇAT.—White Cock. Tapestry. Private Collection.

In renewing the ancient technique of tapestry, Lurçat has found a personal style which restores a poetic and plastic value to visible appearances.

François Desnoyer.—Flowers. Private Collection.
Starting with Cubism, Desnoyer's art borders on reality to the point where it sometimes even yields docilely to actual appearances.

GEORGE GROSZ.—The Market. Private Collection.

Social drama, misery, revolution, and war have continually inspired the art of George Grosz.

THE SCHOOL OF PARIS VERSUS EUROPEAN ART

The increasing fame which the Impressionists and their successors enjoyed throughout Europe enabled Paris to recapture its lost prestige. Superseding the main artistic centers of the foregoing century, such as Rome and Munich, toward 1900 the city began to assume her position as the artistic capital of the world.

Confident of an intelligent reception, enjoying an atmosphere of freedom and the yardstick of international comparisons, foreigners flocked in increasing numbers. Their presence in itself, their enthusiastic curiosity stimulated, in the cafés of Montparnasse and the Butte, friendly exchanges in surroundings especially favorable to ardent discussion.

If some of these artists made brief visits from which they gleaned only

OSKAR KOKOSCHKA.—Portrait of Mr. Hauer.   Private Collection.

The broken modeling, the intermittent line, and the hashed treatment express the dramatic violence which deeply troubled the soul of the Austrian Kokoschka.

transient ideas, many others settled here, finding in Paris a justification of their profession which their own countries were slower to acknowledge.

From one year to the next, this movement gained in breadth. Cut short, dislocated by the war of 1914, it resumed shortly afterwards augmented by the accretions of the war period. The sudden multiplication of galleries, the new speculation in art values were a supplementary attraction. Even the crisis of 1930 was but a temporary setback. Similarly, we see today, after these terrible years of war and distress, how Paris has again won the battle by gradually regrouping around herself her faithful adherents such as Chagall, Ernst, Miro and others, who, victims of circumstances, had been forced to take refuge in the United States or in their homelands.

Among the foreign artists, certain names have been so long and closely associated with Parisian life—names like Picasso, Gris, Kupka, Modigliani, Soutine, Pascin and Chagall—that to-day they pass as natives. Having actively participated in the various movements and excercized great influence, it becomes difficult to pick them out in order to re-insert them in that general classification which encompasses so much: the School of Paris. For how many other artists such as Mondrian and Kandinsky were led by taste, circumstances or displacements to spend not only long periods in Paris but actually whole segments of their lives?

It is undeniable that over the last half-century there have been no hotly-debated causes in the picture world that have not eventually been fought out in Paris, just as there exists no genuine reputation which has not been definitively confirmed here. Rare indeed were those trends which escaped the dominance of Paris. Which is not to say that Paris, in turn, was not the gainer from such genuine foreign contributions as the Ballets Russes or the Munich style.

About 1900, in all the countries of Central and Eastern Europe, a kind of æsthetic fever preyed on people's minds. Cézanne, Gauguin, Van Gogh became the ideals of a unanimous and discerning audience. Collectors, museum directors fought for their canvases, before long to compete for the works of the Fauves and, following that phase, of the Cubists. The latter, little-appreciated in Paris, were shown almost simultaneously in Berlin and Moscow, where they awakened spontaneous interest. This was, indeed, the moment when the famous Shchukine and Morosov Collections were formed in Moscow. When, in 1905, Matisse organized his Paris academy, it was largely German and Scandinavian students who enrolled. In 1907, the Moscow exhibition called "The Crown" assembled the works of the Fauves; while in 1910 in Munich, and 1912 under the ægis of "Der Sturm" in Berlin and of the "Sonderbund" in Cologne, the Cubists and their followers were reunited.

The two sets of currents which alternately blossomed abroad originated almost entirely in outgrowths of either Fauvism or Cubism. However, they were quick to define themselves and turn toward extreme forms, one branch culminating in Expressionism, the other in pure abstraction.

Germany, the country of unquenchable romanticism and pantheism, which clung so tenaciously to the Baroque, was the logical place for the Expressionist current first to appear in force. The artists who made their initial bow in Dresden in 1906 under the name "Die Brücke" (The Bridge) were so conscious of their mission that they more than lived up to this title. For them color and form alone were charged with transmitting the painter's emotion and speaking with authority to the onlooker Exploiting in this way the heritage of Gauguin, they were not above imitating him in his taste for crafts, as illustrated in his crude woodcuts. Two of them, Nolde and Pechstein, both representative figures in the group, went so far as to follow his example and live during the year 1914 among the smaller South Sea islands.

The tragic events experienced by Germany following her defeat reaffirmed the power of Expressionism, which attained, especially with Georg Grosz, a kind of paroxism of ferocity—expression pushed to maximum intensity and dramatic starkness.

Austrian by birth and spirit, Kokoschka for many years lived in retirement, although his name was well known. More spiritual, though basically disturbed by nature, he was above all passionately analytical, vigilantly observant, insatiable in his curiosity. His stay in Dresden from 1918 to 1924, which put him in touch with the German art current, incited him to greater violence both in his color and his technique. From then on, he dedicated himself to a kind of tormented lyricism which, however, is always keyed by elegance and a very personal refinement.

Chagall it was who, while sojourning in Berlin, sealed the bond between Petersburg and Paris. The large exhibition which he had held in the German capital just prior to the war had profound repercussions.

From Germany, and thus indirectly from France, Expressionism propagated itself with varying degrees of rapidity through the other European countries, at times finding specially fertile soil, as in Holland and, still more, Belgium.

But even in Holland, it was Gauguin who was the principle influence on an artist like Sluyters upon his dazzled return from his 1906 trip to Paris. Soon a whole coterie was drawn after him along a line in which mysticism played an equal role with experimentation in distortion. Accompanying this was an urge to challenge reality and a certain brutal irony which made for animated give and take among the Belgian painters. Having lived more or less out of the main stream in Laethem-Saint-Martin, a number of them took refuge during the war in Holland where, thanks to Sluyters and his friends, they came in contact with both German and French Expressionists such as Campendonck and Le Fauconnier. The spark had been struck. Gustave de Smet advanced resolutely in the field of bold simplifications, stylized construction and all the tonal violence of a primarily emotional language—one which, in time, was to find a quieter solution.

This path had been so well paved by the genius of Ensor that Permeke in turn, although a refugee in England, arrived at similar conclusions.

FRANZ MARC.—Blue Horses. Berlin Museum.

Using the Cubist processes of cutting up forms, Marc wished to express the dynamic quality of animal life; horses constitute the favorite subject of his painting.

GUSTAVE DE SMET.—Landscape. Private Collection.
The Fleming De Smet finds his inspiration in popular arts and expresses the rusticity of peasant life.

CONSTANT PERMEKE.—Bride and Bridegroom. Private Collection.
His Flemish peasant types furnish the Belgian Permeke with a pretext to present simple humanity in all its brute force.

Behind him, justifying him, was the whole of the Flemish tradition. Permeke, indeed, reveled in its homely banter, its surly affection for the humble, for country life, for fishermen, which, however, does not excuse him from occasional excesses in this direction.

Leo Gestel.—Portrait of Olga Lassofska. Regnault Collection.

The Dutch painter Gestel seeks in peasant types the principles of a robust and wholesome art, but he does not have the dramatic force which the Fleming Permeke imparts to his rustic pictures.

In the Northern countries, we see the same awakening of a national and popular character. Preceded by the creative contribution of Munch, Expressionism developed freely. Munch's art, related to the School of Pont-Aven in its synthesis, its starkness, its decorative re-arrangement,

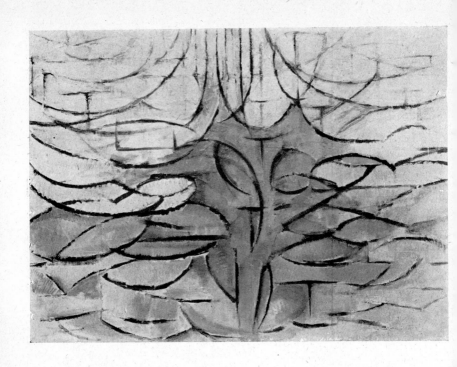

MONDRIAN.—Apple Tree.   The Hague, Gemeentemuseum.

The Dutchman Mondrian has carried "anti-naturalism" right up to mathe-
matical abstraction ; this picture, which is the stylization of the leaf of a tree,
is one of his rare works which owes its inspiration to Nature.

its color sense, initiated a new pictural awareness in Norway.   But Munch's
expression is softened, relaxed, generous.   To the Fauves, more than any
others he acknowledges a debt—especially to Matisse, who transmitted
to his Scandinavian pupils his own taste for color and exact balance.   The
best of these—Per Krogh in Norway and Grünewald in Sweden—divided
their time between Paris and their own countries.   More faithful to his
native Denmark, perhaps by reason of his greater age, Willumsen was
beholden to Gauguin for a brilliant youthful friendship.   In Switzerland,
the older generation co-founder of "Die Brücke," Cuno Amiet, and, still more
Auberjonois, contributed to Expressionism.

One single country escaped this general law of attraction.   This was
Spain.   She could afford this apparent negatiou in that her citizens were

Jan Sluyters.—Nude Woman.   The Hague, Gemeentemuseum.
Elegant and dramatic in turn, the art of the Dutchman Sluyters sometimes
recalls that of his compatriot Van Dongen, who joined with the School of Paris.

EDWARD MUNCH.—The Dead Mother. Museum of Bremen.

The Norwegian Munch, who spent the greater part of his career in Germany, conceived an Expressionist simplification much like that which the Fauves invented in France at the same time.   He had a great influence on the birth of Germanic Expressionism.

flocking in increasing numbers to Paris to augment the Spanish colony and, without denying ther inherent character, eventually forget their true nationality in the cosmopolitan city. At this moment, however, without outside stimulus, Solana introduced into Spain a personal form of Expressionism completely at home in an environment which, by tradition, had always tended in this direction. Guided by instinct alone, Solana describes humanity truculently and with imagination, intermingling sordid and dramatic elements.

It was not long before the compulsion of Cubism began to stimulate in the great European capitals movements similar to itself, at least at their outset. Germany was the first to absorb herself in the problems of formal construction, plastic organization and rhythmic experiment such as Cézanne and Seurat, then Matisse, Picasso and Braque had pioneered. As usual, she carried the argument into her preferred realms, indulging a taste for the illimitable, metaphysics and the cult of the unconscious. The Russian or Eastern elements which at this time were in ascendant merely served to underscore this tendency. They are notable among the artists who, in Munich in 1912, founded the "Blaue Reiter." The latter, although at first submitting to the discipline of Fauvism and Cubism which the majority of the group's founders had methodically followed or exploited, soon rallied around an almost opposite formula which rehabilitated instinct and laid itself open to intuition pure and simple. Kandinsky, who took up a firm position in this line, thus becoming the movement's leading figure (his book and manifesto written in collaboration with Franz Marc were widely read) drew into his wake his friend Marc, Macke and Klee, the last-mentioned more familiar with French methods and in closer contact with Paris.

In these works, dislocation operates more on the spiritual plane than might at first blush seem apparent, Marc and Macke attempting at all times to combine constructional rules with their visionary sense. Following the recurrent Germanic yearning for an absolute metaphysics, Kandinsky in 1911 abandoned all recourse to nature and advocated the purest abstraction as a means of delivering himself from reality—that is, acceptance of the dictates of the subconscious alone. Actuated by his Slavic temperament, full of instinctive élan and sublimated urge to commune with the universal, he made maximum use of inorganic forms and colors, endowing them with an appearance of spontaneous effusion and lyric polyphony.

In France, at the same time, we find Villon and Kupka, the latter referring back to his Czech origins, and finally Delaunay, who had close bonds with Marc and Macke, ending no less in abstraction although, by contrast, they retained a strict plastic construction more suited to the uses of pure intelligence.

The same is true of the Italian Futurists who, reacting to the manifesto that Marinetti had just published in Paris, constituted themselves as a

CARLO CARRA.—Metaphysical Still-Life. Puzzolini Collection.

Like his compatriot Chirico during his Surrealist phase, Carlo Carra arranges objects without any apparent relation, in order to create an atmosphere of mystery.

group in 1910. Boccioni and his friends, who first turned up in Paris, like the Cubists made an effort to dissolve reality and extract from it a logical, formal architecture. More engrossed than Braque or Picasso by problems

UMBERTO BOCCIONI.—Study of a Head. The Mother. Private Collection.
By his process of fragmenting objects, the Italian Boccioni, animator of the Futurist group, tried to express the dynamic aspect of life.

of time and rhythm, they diverged from the Cubist tradition out of desire to integrate the movement.

Similarly, we see in Czechoslovakia and especially in Holland and Russia artists taking a more and more independent stand. If it is via his Slavic inheritance that Filla escaped the bonds of Cubism, the Dutch Neo-Plasticists, together with "de Stijl" (a publication founded in 1927) approached pictural problems from the angle of rational experiment thanks to the

GIORGIO DI CHIRICO.—Horses on the Seashore. Paul Guillaume Collection.

In his latest period, which belongs to the Italian School, Giorgio di Chirico discards the surrealist symbolism of his early manner to seek inspiration from antiquity.

VASSILI KANDINSKY.—Landscape. Private Collection.
Kandinsky conceived an art of signs and symbols much more abstract than Cubism, for its forms take nothing from Nature.

spiritual direction of Mondrian. Reducing his formula from schematized plan to mere blue-print, this artist reached the outermost limits of painting, ending up with a kind of æsthetic crystallization in bright-colored rhythms which excludes all subjectivity. Superficially opposed to the intuitive approach of the German abstractionists, this art actually resembles theirs in its typically Nordic search for the symbolism of forms and numbers.

The Russians reflect an allied point of view which, developed with characteristic fanaticism a succession of rival schools all of which, however, endorse an identical liberation of the senses and mystic cult for dynamism and abstract space.

With the Suprematist Malewitch religiously tracing his black square on black, we approach the realm of paradox. A little later, following the end of the war, Constructivism with Moholy-Nagy proclaimed new conquests of form which the Puvsner brothers were to pursue in sculpture and which had strong repercussions in Germany where, from 1920 on, the flourishing Bauhaus movement began to attract the leading Abstractionists of the day.

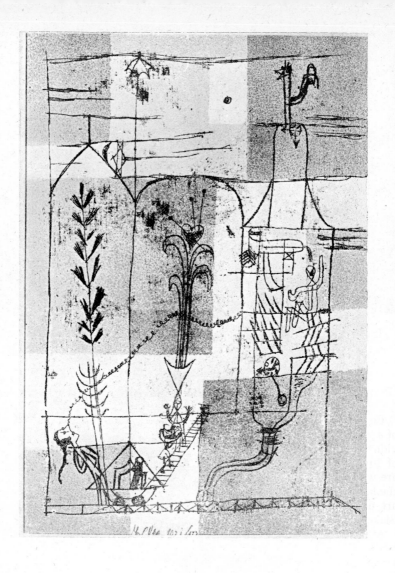

PAUL KLEE.—Scene, from "Tales of Hoffman." Private Collection.

By taking his inspiration from children's drawings and the graphism of uncivilized arts, the Swiss painter Paul Klee believes he can rediscover the magic writing of the primitives.

W. R. SICKERT.—Venice.   London, Tate Gallery.

CONTEMPORARY ENGLISH PAINTING

English contemporary painting presents a paradox: the total absence of a general national style demonstrated in oils and watercolors whose individuality could only have developed in the British Isles.   The basic elements of Impressionism, Fauvism and abstraction came from abroad; but they are woven into patterns that are local and personal.   On the other hand, the latent Romanticism of the British national character revives in modern art under new forms which, in their way, are as mystical as Palmer or Blake.

At the outset of the century, Impressionism was the adventurous style. Walter Sickert, the devoted pupil and admirer of Whistler, the friend of Degas, had worked extensively on the Continent, especially in Dieppe. But the clear tones of the *plein-airistes* are altered in his pictures by the subdued light of England.   His street scenes present a pervading golden-brown.   For Sickert remained an English painter despite the charm of his Dieppe canvases and the magnificence of the paintings done in Venice, in

P. WILSON STEER.—Seated Nude.   London, Tate Gallery.

A solid, honest figure piece by the leading landscapist of the early part of the century.   The broad paint style, a heritage of Constable, is typical of the older English moderns.

P. WILSON STEER.—Interior.   Private Collection.

Modified Impressionism, a pervasive influence in England around 1900, is evident in the overall flicker of Steer's canvases.   The quiet intimacy of this scene compares with the work of Bonnard.

ETHEL WALKER.—The Fishergirl.   Collection of the artist's family.

A delicate, feminine color sense is offset in the work of Dame Ethel Walker by masculine firmness of touch, as evidenced in the broad, sure laying in of this characterful head.

which St. Marks glows with Byzantine splendor of coloring, echoing the gold mosaics within. Many of his most characteristic pictures are of the Old Bedord Theatre in Camden Town, a poor district of London, where he lived for some years. Sickert had once considered becoming an actor himself, and his scenes of the tense audience crowding the top galleries of the music hall, absorbed and enchanted by the glitter of the stage below, have the glamor and excitement of true theater. He also painted bedroom scenes, enjoying the contrast between these meager surroundings and the beauty he could extract from such unpromising material.

Philip Wilson Steer was the son of a portrait painter, brought up in the Wye Valley amid some of the loveliest scenery in England. After some study in Gloucester, he went to Paris, and there worked first at Julian's and afterwards at the Beaux-Arts. He, too, could not fail to be affected by the rapidly expanding influence of the French Impressionists. Some of his early pictures show this French influence to a marked degree.

Basically, however, Wilson Steer was no cosmopolitan. After working in Paris for two years, he returned to England and, from then on, the great English landscape painters Constable and Turner were his real masters. But where the latter was able to soar into the far realms of the imagination, bringing to his painting something of Claude's richness and golden light, Steer could follow only at a distance. His landscapes are most satisfactory when he least tries to emulate the Romanticism of his master and takes the quieter path of Constable.

Steer painted some charming portraits and made attempts at figure composition which have not, however, the strength and accomplishment of his landscapes. Late in life his eyesight began to fail, and he concentrated on watercolors, laying in the essentials of the landscapes before him in broad washes, none the less effective and sensitive if much of the detail escaped him.

A woman who achieved great distinction in her painting, which is frankly of the Impressionnist school, is Ethel Walker. In her youth, she was influenced by Oriental art and later conceived an admiration for Whistler. With no stereotyped art education, she worked a great deal in museums, and only at 35 went to art school. Eventually she became a pupil of Walter Sickert. There is nothing hit-or-miss about her work; it has a sureness of touch and a solid grasp of form which is very impressive. It is this underlying solidity which sets off the shimmering quality of her landscapes and seascapes. Her tones are all in the lightest key. She makes great use of white, some of her paintings being literally symphonies in white. Having the capacity to work quickly, she sustains the general tone of the work with remarkable consistency throughout.

Another painter, who worked under the influence of the French Impres-

FRANCES HODGKINS.—The Valley Mill.   Winchester, Eric Lucas Collection.

One of England's most gifted woman painters, Frances Hodgkins exploits the mobility of shape, the interplay of color, weaving out of both a two-dimensional tapestry of individuality and charm.

sionists, is New Zealand born Frances Hodgkins.   Renoir, Manet and Sisley were her favorite painters when, after an extended period of study and a teaching career in Paris, she took up permanent residence in England.

As she progressed away from her Impressionist manner, her painting became a fascinating admixture of tones, superimposed one over the other, complementing each other by brilliant patches.   Out of the general mass of color, the forms emerge semi-abstracted.

Frances Hodgkins was able to create this effect both with watercolor

VICTOR PASMORE.—Parisian Café.   Manchester, City Art Gallery.

Youngest of the group indebted to Impressionism, this artist reconstituted its technique into a personal, diaphanous style.   Pasmore is a modern in his regrouping of subject, his bold departures from nature.

and oils, but because of the thinness and the lack of definition of the latter, she is never quite as satisfactory in this medium.

Whatever subject she touched, whether landscape, still-life, portraits or figure composition, she imbued with her peculiar vision.   Living among northern mists made her visits to the brilliant sun of the Mediterranean even more invigorating.   When the war of 1939 forced her to remain in England, she began to interest herself in the countryside around her. Farmyard scenes and farm implements inspired her to some of her most animated work.   She continued to paint with undiminished vigor till her death in 1947.

A latent conservatism in the English character, in art as in other matters, has made many of to-day's critics and amateurs of painting long for the easier surface attractions of the Impressionist school. While despising the imitation of much academic work, they feel that in Victor Pasmore they have found a latter-day painter who can still combine individuality with something of the Impressionist charm.

During his career as a civil servant he was for many years a Sunday painter, going to evening art classes and working week-ends and during his holidays. In the end he freed himself and emerged as an artist with a character of his own. His pictures have a predominantly Impressionist feeling, but they also have balance of color and solidity despite blurred contours and melting of tone into tone. His subjects are Impressionist favorites : quiet domestic scenes, figures sitting at a table with a lamp, a girl sewing, a few flowers in a glass. Yet Pasmore does not seem altogether satisfied with his victories in this field and is looking about for other forms of expression. At one moment, a strong Whistler influence began to appear in his pictures, superimposing a Japanese character on the misty English landscape. Later, he tried his hand at abstract designs in which he retained the softness of his Impressionist color range.

It might seem that it is too difficult for an eager and lively artist to-day to confine his personality within the framework of the Impressionist tradition, but Pasmore has established himself in England as a leading painter in this now almost historical style.

Sir William Nicholson is an artist whom it is difficult to relate to any school. His painting might be called academic, with the academism of the late 19th century, yet its distinction and individuality lift it above mere traditional work. He has a strong sense of design, a sense of form and great skill in his craft. This feeling for design helped him when he took to creating posters and woodcuts.

Woodcuts, posters and book illustration were but one facet of Nicholson's art. In his portraits, there are greys which remind one of Manet, without, however, Manet's freedom of touch. When looking at his still-lifes, Chardin is brought even more strongly to mind. There is something here of the quiet forcefulness of the great still-life painter, the delicacy of tone and the steadiness of vision which can regard simple objects with such clarity that they isolate them in space and present them to us with new meaning.

While Sickert and Ethel Walker were carrying on in England the tradition of the French Impressionist school and Steer was trying to return to the Constable and Turner tradition, Augustus John was exploiting academicism with a force and bravura that gained him immediate attention. He was a brilliant student. Both his personality and striking appearance fitted

WILLIAM NICHOLSON.—Still-life with a Melon.   Roland Browse
Delbanco Collection.

*There is something bluff and uncompromising about the work of this artist who,
in an academic technique, manages to say more than the obvious about his
subject, whether portrait or still-life.*

him to fulfil the role of artist in the popular imagination, even without his
precocious technical accomplishment.

Some of John's early pictures of Wales, with figures of women in gipsy
kerchiefs, have a distinction and sensitivity not always apparent in his
later work.   As a portrait painter, he shows a strength of drawing and a
massive modeling in brushwork which makes the accomplishment of other
contemporary successful portraitists look weak and amateurish.   His picture of Lawrence of Arabia, in the Tate Gallery, is a fine study of an
exceptional man, and his portrait head of the poet Yeats also expresses
something of the quality of the great Irishman.   Perhaps at his finest when
using a pencil, he has done a great many drawings of fluency and grace
—items much sought after by collectors.

AUGUSTUS JOHN.—Mother and Child. Private Collection.

Leading figure of England's pre-moderns, John infects his subjects with his own vitality. Working within an academic tradition, his concept is fresh, his modeling in broad brushstrokes is virtuoso.

GWEN JOHN.—Self-Portrait.   London, Tate Gallery.
The sister of Augustus John, her approach is more feminine, less for effect.
Devoid of props, starkly frontal, this portrait reveals her insight into personality,
her uncompromising attitude toward herself.

DUNCAN GRANT.—The Bathers. Australia, Gallery of Victoria.

Influenced through his friend Roger Fry along the line of Cézanne's experiments, Grant was preoccupied by rhythm and the relation of forms, eventually earning secondary laurels as a decorative artist.

Gwen John, Augustus John's sister, was of an opposite nature to her brother and this is apparent in her painting. Sensitive, retiring, quiet, her pictures pitched in a low key, have all the delicate sensibility inherent in her personality. Her drawing is free and Impressionistic in quality. Her paintings are few and on a small scale, but her *Lady Reading a Book*, in the Tate Gallery, is not readily forgotten.

Between 1900 and 1920, the art critic Roger Fry exerted a great influence in England, bringing to the attention of the public the importance of the

Post-Impressionist movement across the Channel. Due to him the first Post-Impressionist exhibition was held in London in 1910. This was an epoch-making event in contemporary English art. To many artists, especially the younger painters, the exhibition was a revelation. Among these was Duncan Grant. Through family connections, he was early in contact with a group of lively intellects, including, among others, his cousin, Lytton Strachey, the writer; Virginia Woolf, the novelist; Maynard Keynes, the economist and an enthusiastic patron of the arts; and Roger Fry himself. This circle is often referred to as the Bloomsbury group, because some of its members lived in the neighborhood of Bloomsbury Square in London. Their opinions became influential and they helped create a body of public opinion capable of appreciating what was going on in Paris.

Duncan Grant worked through this phase and it was as an apostle of the newer school of painting, then developing in Paris, that he made such a strong impression on many of the most advanced art connoisseurs in England before the 1914 war.

From these early paintings, it was at once apparent that Grant was a born decorator and that the gaiety and lightness of his touch had an extraordinary charm. Roger Fry was aware of this gift in his friend and when he started the Omega workshop for the production and sale of applied art Duncan Grant was at once involved. He designed printed linens and carpets, painted screens, tables and pottery.

Perhaps it was the natural ease with which he created his designs that made Duncan Grant take stock as to his ultimate intentions as a painter of pictures. In these his style has changed progressively with the years as he concentrated more and more on solidity of form. His color is arbitrary, his harmonies are surprising. Little by little, Grant has moved away from his earlier French influences and taken on something of the stolidity of the English countryside in which he lives.

Despite his upbringing in the coldly English atmosphere of Yorkshire, Matthew Smith's painting has absorbed the warmth and color of Provence where he has spent so much of his time. For it was in France that he learned to paint, working for a short time with Matisse, and it was from the Fauves that he took his brilliant and burning color. Matthew Smith paints in reds and blues and greens; vermilion and rose madder predominate in his pictures. His drawing is as violent as his coloring, broad and uncompromising, with the strength of a man who, having made up his own mind, puts down his conclusions with a decision that brooks no argument.

When he paints a nude she is frequently shown on a crimson coverlet, the flesh all dark Venetian red and ochers, never rising to high lights. Matthew Smith does not seem to need high lights. Though his drawing is free, there is no superficiality about his pictures. There has been no

MATTHEW SMITH.—Reflection.   Private Collection.

wide divergence in his style since first, by dint of much labor and difficulty, he was able to put his personality on his canvas.

Owing to the shortness of his life, Christopher Wood must be classed as belonging to the 1920's.   He died at the early age of 29, but had he lived, he might have become one of the most important painters of his generation.

Wood was greatly influenced by the School of Paris, and in all his pictures can be detected influences of this or that contemporary painter whose work he admired.   Whereas this is a weakness of immaturity passed through by nearly all creative artists, Christopher Wood, at the same time, had already discovered a manner unmistakably his own.   Whenever this style predominated over the other elements in his mind, he painted pictures which seem to be the prelude to great achievements.

His paintings of Brittany are particularly pleasing, whether of landscape, boats in harbor or peasants dancing in a market place.   The pink and yellow

CHRISTOPHER WOOD.—Breton Village. London, Lefevre Gallery.

Despite a technique, palette and subject matter derived from France, where he spent formative years, Christopher Wood retained an infinitely promising artistic individuality to which his untimely death put an end.

houses, the brilliant blue-green sea, the massed masts and rigging of boats are felt experiences, not just surface appearances noted down by an observant eye. When Christopher Wood was killed by falling in front of an express train a career of great promise was tragically terminated.

Another link between the arts of England and the Continent is Ben Nicholson, the son of Sir William Nicholson. In reaction against his conventional family art circle, it was not until he went to Paris and saw the work of the Cubists that he suddenly knew in which direction his own road must take him.

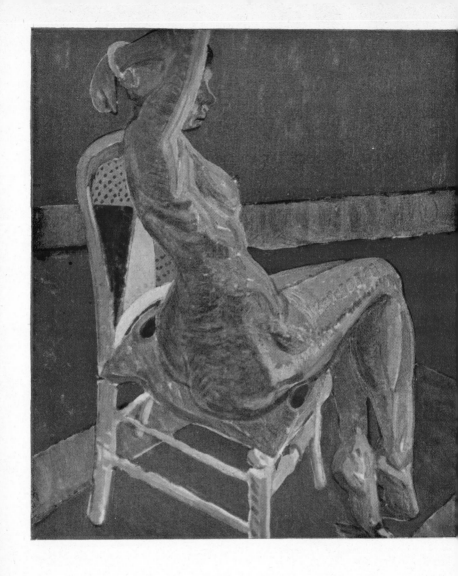

MATTHEW SMITH.—No. 1 Fitzroy Street. A. J. L. McDonnell Collection.
*Impassioned exponent of the Fauve arbitrary color theory, Matthew Smith
differs from them in his living, unstylized drawing expressed in his forms.*

STANLEY SPENCER.—The Lovers or The Dustmen. Newcastle-on-Tyne,
Lanig Art Gallery.

*Purposeful, stylized yet exuberant in his distortions, this artist indulges a
sophisticated form of primitivism which sometimes approaches the grotesque,
yet is always moving and understandable to his large audience.*

From 1926 to 1933 he painted pictures which have a close relationship
to the work of Picasso and Braque in the 1920's, but they also have a very
individual charm of their own. If they lack some of the energy of the
paintings by the Paris masters, they have a quietness of color and feeling which recalls the stillness that pervades the painting of Piero della
Francesca. But the reticence even of such delicate painting as this, was

PAUL NASH.—Landscape of the Vernal Equinox.
Collection of Her Majesty the Queen.

Painter of two wars, Nash filtered his experiences into a mystical worship of nature, of the equinoxes, of meteorological events. His cool, dispassionate color lends these themes a haunting quality.

not enough. Ben Nicholson probed even further into the possibilities of a purely abstract art. Circles and intersecting lines of uncompromising severity became the basis of his art. His color also became harder, each tone being separated rigidly from the next and only sometimes were the delicate textures and subtly blended colors of his earlier work allowed to intrude.

But the artist himself seems to have found that such a severe discipline of line and values was unable to contain all that he needed to express. By degrees the earlier personality is emerging once more and certain landscape motives show a realistic note which is more typically English.

Stanley Spencer is an artist who need make no claim to being an English painter, for his art could hardly have been created anywhere outside of

England. True to a strong realistic tendency in British art, from Hogarths, painting of the *Rake's Progress* through the Pre-Raphaelites, his pictures tell a story.

The Bible has been the great single stimulus to this artist's imagination, and after that, the village of Cookham in Berkshire where he lived. When he paints Christ carrying the Cross, then this cross progresses through the village street of Cookham, and men and women rise from their broken graves in Cookham churchyard. This naïve approach is sufficiently genuine to be acceptable as a direct expression and not merely as an attempt to imitate the attitude of mind of Giotto and the early Florentines.

Spencer uses an exaggerated perspective and an odd distortion of the human figure, sustained throughout all his painting so that his work is quite unmistakable. The 1914-1918 war also had a powerful effect on him as an artist, resulting in a chapel where he depicted something of this great experience. Built at Burghclere in Berkshire, Spencer decorated the whole interior with murals showing the life of soldiers on campaign, and, on the east wall, a great picture of the Resurrection. This is one of the most important war memorials, and represents the painter's major creative work.

In Paul Nash we find another painter whose work has real English individuality and character. For Paul Nash, the 1914-1918 war was a shattering experience in a world that had seemed reasonably safe and ordered. Up to that time, he had been painting pleasantly Impressionistic pictures which he showed with the New English Art Club. After his experiences in the trenches, the stark shapes and coldly unnatural colors of his *Sanctuary Wood, Dawn 1917* or *Menin Road, 1918* rank not merely as landscapes, but an expression of the horror created in the minds of men to whom the wilful destruction of nature brought an even more violent reaction than the destruction of man by man. Through his war pictures, Paul Nash moved into the front rank of English art, and was commissioned to paint important panels for the Imperial War Museum and the Canadian war records.

At times rigidly geometric, at others full of fantasy, Nash represents a synthesis of the School of Paris influence and the native Romanticism of his countrymen. His cool, delicate colors belong to the grey light of the north. The fitful English sun on the chalk downs, the pale sand dunes, the sea of an indefinite blue melting into the horizon covers the whole range of his palette. Though there is a certain sharpness of geometric forms, there is no violence to these tones.

Toward the end of his life, the artist was preoccupied with landscapes and strange, primeval flowers. His color grew deeper and brighter, a new force and energy seemed to be coming into his work. The development was cut short by his death.

BEN NICHOLSON.—Still-life. London, Tate Gallery.

Bulwark of abstract art in Great Britain, this painter's compositions are seldom coldly mathematical, exhibiting a sensitiveness to texture and frequent whimsicality of form which relate them to living experience.

DAVID JONES.—Lord of Venedetia.   London, Private Collection.

This perceptive artist, in his almost dream-like visions of Celtic myth and legend, excels at delicate coloring and, for all his diffuseness and profusion of elements, at linear pattern.

JOHN PIPER.—The Cathedral. Leicester Gallery.

Whether describing a wild gorge or a castle, Piper brings to his subject a brooding, almost theatrical imagination which has become one of the hallmarks of the new English Romantic movement.

David Jones, brought up in Wlaes, acquired the Celtic love of myth and legend. As a boy he was enthusiastically interested in drawing animals and in book illustration. Thrown into the ordeal of 1914-1918, he emerged deeply marked by the experience. By the time he returned to work in an art school, he was sufficiently mature to appreciate the æsthetic revolution which had taken place in France. The composition of his pictures, his drawing and pale, bright color showed that he had looked sympathetically at the paintings of Matisse and other artists of the School of Paris.

But Jones was no imitator. Pre-eminently a watercolorist, his work was delicate and light, and there was a mystical element about his painting even when his subjects were landscapes or grazing animals. Nearly twenty years after the first World War, he published *In Parentheses*, a book which deals with 1914-1918 experiences and which won the Hawthornden prize in 1938.

His output as a painter was now rather small and when he did paint, the romantic, legendary ideas which he had woven into the realistic details of his book, asserted themselves. Ethereal figures creep into his landscapes, his trees are the trees of an enchanted wood; the buildings are chapels or shrines for some spiritual experience. Echoes of the legend of King Arthur are present everywhere.

Mention must here be made of Edward Burra, for he is also a watercolorist, although he uses the medium in a manner peculiar to himself. Some of his paintings are large and crammed with life-size figures. His work has a definite Surrealist quality, and he has exhibited in various Surrealist exhibitions.

If Burra's attitude to life is cynical and his figures repellent, their grotesqueness is enhanced by the beauty of the color that he uses. A long desired visit to Mexico provides him with stimulus, and his *Interior of a Mexican Church* was bought by the Tate Gallery. Burra spent some time in the United States and did many drawings in Harlem. The exotic atmosphere of colorful Negro life, against the background of New York, appealed to him strongly. His subsequent pictures of odd figures with beak-like noses carry us back to the German painter Grünewald, with whom he now seems to have a strong affinity. In addition to painting, Burra has designed three ballets.

In John Piper and Graham Sutherland, the Romantic spirit of one phase of contemporary British art is eloquently expressed. Piper passed through many phases of artistic development. His early inspiration stemmed from the Continent. His first works are purely decorative, the frame being considered an essential part of the picture as a whole. He did *collages* of considerable charm, using many of the forms tried by Picasso and Braque. A few years later he became an enthusiast for abstract

GRAHAM SUTHERLAND.—Thorn Tree. London, Lefevre Gallery.

Out of natural phenomena, Sutherland has derived a language of spikes and of gnarled and knotted forms which, on the one hand, bespeaks the new Romanticism, on the other, a typically Nordic pantheism.

art, making "objects" out of rods and wire netting with round and angular, broken and unbroken forms. At this time he ran an English magazine devoted to abstract art called *Axis*.

But Piper soon reverted to paint. As a side line, he did many topographical drawings and tracings of stained glass. He also worked on a guide

ROBERT COLQUHOUN.—Woman at a Window.   London,
Richard Smart Collection.

Animated by the School of Paris and Picasso, Colquhoun's works have an
unbeautiful, uncompromising aspect which, despite the artist's youth, has
already proved influential among his generation.

IAN MACBRYDE.—Still-life.   London, Lefèvre Gallery.

Like Colquhoun a young Scottish insurrectionist, MacBryde works in a strik-
ing semi-abstract idiom, is at his best in evocative still-lifes activated by
enigmatic form and grandiose color clashes.

to the county in which he lived and took a great number of photographs
of old buildings (an archæological interest, particularly in the architecture
of old churches, had been a continual interest since boyhood).

Graham Sutherland belongs to that romantic group which, to some critics,

JOHN CRAXTON.—Alderbolt Mill. Peter Watson Collection.

For a period attracted to School of Paris forms, Craxton applies them in this picture to the crystallization of a familiar scene, intensifying its vital quality by broad simplification.

seems the essentially English school. It is an attitude to life which has produced great poetry and placed England foremost in the ranks of literature. Sutherland is interested in natural form—plants or rocks, a broken tree trunk. In a small boulder he can find shapes and color with which to create a whole picture. At another time, he will paint the sun between hills, or a great cliff with a road winding up it.

Meanwhile there are several other young painters who are pursuing a very different form of art. Robert Colquhoun and Ian MacBryde have worked much together and, at first sight, their painting shows a great similarity. They choose the same subjects chiefly preoccupied with figure compositions.

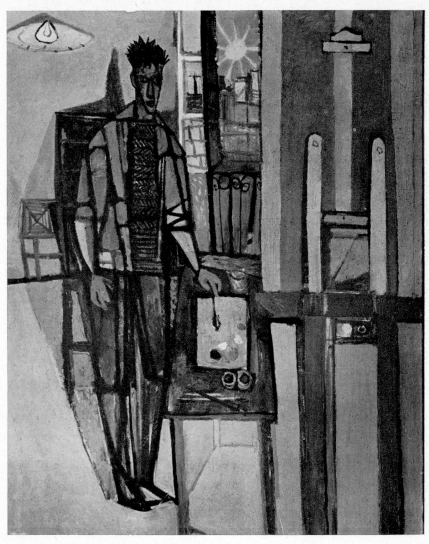

JOHN MINTON.—Self-Portrait. London, Lefevre Gallery.

Built out of dramatic verticals, this picture rests on a firm structural basis, is related not only to contemporary Paris but, in its heavy underscoring of black, to the Expressionists.

EDWARD BURRA.—Birdmen and Mugs.   Private Collection.

*In the terms of a masquerade whose main parts are played by punchinellos,
Burra interprets the satiric, bitter, even savage aspects of modern life.   His
color is as bold as his drawing is vigorous.*

LUCIEN FREUD.—Dead Heron.   F. S. Hess Collection.

This artist, son of the famous psychoanalyst, is the logical exponent of Surrealism in England.   Grotesque or wildly fantastic, his drawings carry conviction in their technical perfection.

The forms are not treated realistically, but are abstracted and built up into monumental figures from whose strange faces melancholy eyes stare out at the onlooker. Neither Colquhoun nor MacBryde makes any concessions to charm or accepted types of beauty.

Another painter, without the forcefulness of Colquhoun, but with a wider range of subject matter, is John Minton. He paints landscapes, figures and still-life.

Other young painters who have attracted attention are Lucien Freud, whose meticulous drawing has a Surrealist quality; and John Craxton, whose undoubted gifts have still not freed themselves from an enthusiastic subservience to great masters.

WILLIAM J. GLACKENS.—The Green Car.   New York, Metropolitan Museum.
*New York was a sprawling, still crude city, when Glackens painted it half a
century ago.   But in addition to nostalgic charm, these pictures have pictorial
authority, carrying through the Eakins tradition to latter-day realists.*

CONTEMPORARY AMERICAN PAINTING

The first decade of 20th century art in America was a postscript to
the 19th.   It was a period of great untaxed fortunes and great houses
filled with Bouguereau nudes, the pastorals of Mauve and Diaz de la
Peña, the portraits of Sargent.   Europe and things European were the
criterion of taste.   The realist contingent which had begun to envision a
sturdier America met with the epithet "Ashcan School" when, in 1908,
eight men banded together under the leadership of the brilliant George
Bellows, Robert Henri the influential teacher, and the forthright John Sloan.
Two other notable names in the group are William Glackens, painter of
New York's shabby flamboyance, and George Luks, who depicted its tough

[285]

GEORGE LUKS.—Otis Skinner as Col. Bridau. Washington, D. C., Phillips Memorial Gallery.—*A leading actor of the period as seen by its greatest characterizer of types. But Luks did not confine himself to top hats, some of his strongest work depicting New York's human flotsam and jetsam.*

JOHN MARIN.—Fifth Avenue and 42nd Street. Washington, D. C.,
Phillips Memorial Gallery.

*The first American Cubist found ideal material, upon his return from Paris,
in New York. Marin, however, soon abandoned his style for a more personal,
dramatic art which found its best expression in watercolor.*

characters, alleys and waterfronts. In general, "The Eight" as they called
themselves, portrayed in paint the unvarnished here-and-now much as
the realist school in literature expressed it in words twenty years later.
To-day they have attained a kind of classicism which makes it hard to
think of them as modern. Historically, they were a recurrence of the
literal strain in American painting which goes back, through Eakins and
Homer, through Catlin and Bingham, to the original journeyman painters,
who gazed so steadily and uncompromisingly at the first American settlers.

Europe continued to beckon, but the accent was beginning to shift.
In 1905, two years before the famous Cézanne retrospective in Paris which

ROBERT HENRI.—Gypsy with a Cigarette. New York, Collection International Business Machines Corp.—*Henri popularized not only the loaded
brush technique, which he acquired while studying in Munich, but picturesque
studio effects such as his European counterparts had affected since the 1850's.*

John Sloan.—Old Clown Making Up.   Washington, D. C., Phillips Memorial Gallery.—*Moving spirit of the "Ashcan" school of realism which devoted itself to depicting life in its more unvarnished aspects, Sloan soon became a powerful influence through pictures such as this.*

GEORGE BELLOWS.—Stage Sharkey (detail). Cleveland Museum of Art.
*Hard-hitting as his celebrated boxing studies, Bellows first introduced sport
as a subject for the painter's brush.   His canvases are paralleled by a remarkable output of graphic art.*

KARL KNATHS.—Harvest.   Washington, D. C., Phillips Memorial Gallery.
Influenced at an early date by Cubism, Knaths developed an independent art based on a balanced, intersecting linear plan.   His once quiet, distinguished color has gained in vivacity over the years.

has been called the birth of modern art, a lanky Yankee-by-adoption called John Marin went abroad, ultimately to sell a picture to the Luxembourg. He had pretty well assimilated the European vision before he returned to rediscover the vitality of his own country.   New York skyscrapers, with their "pushing, pulling forces" he describes in a still new language of dynamic, jumbled cubes.   Later he turned this approach on the Maine coast, with its jagged waves and jutting rocks.   So oracular are these pictures that, in the year 1950, John Marin remains modern without having materially changed his style.   To-day he has achieved an old-master status, a must in the purchasing list of any up-to-date museum.

Stuart Davis.—New York Waterfront. Buffalo, Albright Art Gallery.
America's pioneer abstractionist, this painter's art has gained steadily since his first appearance with the Armory Show. Full of dynamism, precise in color balance, his patterns have also ornamented textiles.

Max Weber is another painter who, before 1910, came under the influence of Cézanne during a trip abroad.   Today his work has a more Expressionist bent and, in its passion, in his choice of Hebrew types and improbable female figures, it can be compared with that of Soutine, while Weber's opalescent greys, impetuous blacks and weeping landscapes at times recall Vlaminck.   If completely dissociated with American life today, he has exerted a strong influence on the younger American Expressionists.

Another artist for whom Cubism was a guiding force is Karl Knaths. Exercising great natural gifts within the strict angles of its lore, Knaths manages to bring the lifting touch of poetry to such subjects as duck decoys, harbor scenes, lilacs.   His good fortune in having an early museum-director patron has little to do with the real achievement of his career.

MAX WEBER.—Summer. New York, Whitney Museum of American Art.
Weber's use of distortion, which, from this lyrical application of 1917, has developed in an emotional Expressionist direction, has no counterpart (though many echoes) in American painting.   His color is infinitely subtle.

The big event to which these early attempts are linked, and which crystallised many styles into a new idiom, was the Armory Show. By 1913, a few artists, such as Walt Kuhn and Stuart Davis, determined to shock America into action by showing her how retrogressive her artistic taste was.   Kuhn went abroad, where Davis joined him, requisitioned Cézannes,

WALT KUHN.—The Blue Juggler. Kansas City, Mo., William Rockhill Nelson Gallery.

Although a chief organizer of the radical 1913 Armory Show, Kuhn in his own art stuck close to appearances, realizing the truth of his vision in analytical studies of clowns and jugglers and distinguished still-lifes.

Yasuo Kuniyoshi.—I'm Tired.   New York, Whitney Museum of American Art.—*In its subtlety, the art of this Japanese-American often defies classification though in turn it was formalized and romantically expressive. Kuniyoshi's palette, centered on diaphanous greys, is infinitely eloquent.*

CHARLES SHEELER.—Offices. Washington, D. C., Phillips Memorial Gallery.

The geometric forms of American industrial life inspired Sheeler; his second profession of photography dictated the smooth, nuanceless texture of his paintings. His analysis is impersonal but never cold.

Van Goghs, Matisses, Redons, Brancusis and, finally, Marcel Duchamp's *Nude Descending the Staircase*, which became the conversation piece among some 1,100 works. Included were many Americans who heretofore had lacked precedent in experiment. Before it broke up, the Armory Show traveled to Chicago and Boston, opening eyes to the fact that a great many people saw things differently.

It was around this time that an adventurous gallery came to the fore, the "291" Photo-Secession gallery (later called An American Place) where John Marin first exhibited. Its guiding spirit, Alfred Stieglitz, pioneered in demanding recognition of photography as a fine art. Stieglitz's early string of artists included Marsden Hartley and Georgia O'Keeffe. Like Marin's, Hartley's subject was Maine. Its Mount Khatadin, its granite seacoast, its pounding cascading surf he formalised with utmost vigor and dramatic use of black. An iron fate as well as a cold climate seems to bind his figures. His color is handsome: black, rich brown, dark red, deep cold blue and chilling foamy white. Georgia O'Keeffe, a school-teacher from Wisconsin and Texas who eventually became Stieglitz's wife, also formalises American material, but by refining, polishing, drawing myopically close to plant details or the dried bones of the Southwest until they blot out her canvas and take on new and compelling significance. Hartley and O'Keeffe assimilated the Paris influence, if not at first hand, as part of the new stirrings of curiosity. They pioneered for a number of other artists who hit their stride somewhere between dispassionate abstraction and photographic reporting. Purifying and editing, they distilled the essence of the country (not to be confused with the subsequent American Scene painters who rendered these same things literally). This abbreviating process came naturally to the Japanese-American Kuniyoshi. His early paintings, with their tweaked forms, their glossy browns and blacks, have utmost lilt and style. Charles Demuth, who early came in contact with the Gertrude Stein group in Paris, took similar liberties with things seen. At times his outline is capriciously free, at others, sternly simple, forshadowing Charles Sheeler. This latter is a deliberate craftsman whose paintings were strongly influenced by his second career, photography. In the 1920's he depicted the bold hulks of Pennsylvania barns, later the pure inhumanity of factory forms. Sheeler edits details which do not interest him, then endows his main forms with ultimate descriptiveness. In a cold palette which never strays far from black-grey-white, his gradations of tone are delicate. Milton Avery, as the first American Fauve, also played an important role in the period when America was learning from Europe. A quiet, almost plodding worker at his problems of balancing flat color areas, he developed a personal, sensitive art which has hardly received its due as one of the signposts of the 20th century.

CHARLES DEMUTH.—Eggplants. Washington, D. C.,
Phillips Memorial Gallery.

One of the most original talents in the early years of American modernism,
Demuth is noted for still-lifes whose glassy facets indicate a debt to Cubism
and for brilliant, analytical book illustrations.

While repercussions of the Armory Show spread over the country in
widening circles, while artists cu ltivated the seed of new ideals, one contingent stuck to the notion that the painter's contract with his public was
to represent things as they looked. Oddly, Walt Kuhn, who had hand-
picked the revolutionary Armory Show, stands out to-day as not only the
most loyal, but perhaps the most important exponent of this philosophy.
Kuhn's circus folk combine clear descriptions of height, width, color,
outline, physiognomy with a deeply intuitive element. His paint is broad
and rich and without bravura tricks. He sets himself difficult tasks: an
uncompromising head-on angle, an unprepossessing light, repetitive material
(it also extended to still-life and an occasional landscape). Instead of
changing as was the fashion, he strove over the years to better himself
with in this range.

Guy Pène du Bois, of a French New Orleans family, also painted with
intent to reproduce what he saw. Expert gradations veil his color, a satiri-

MARSDEN HARTLEY.—Nova Scotia Fishermen. New York,
Collection International Business Machines Corp.

*Out of American folk themes, such as the fishermen of the northern coast,
Hartley created a vigorous art in which schematic conventionalizations were
keyed up to an almost Expressionist degree of intensity.*

MILTON AVERY.—Brown Hat.   Private Collection.

*Boldly silhouetted shapes and simplified accounts of texture constitute the pic-
tural language of Milton Avery.   Once a Fauve, he still practices the school's
arbitrary color within a personal style.*

EUGENE SPEICHER.—Graziana. Private Collection.

Its rapid brush effortlessly conveying the texture of flesh and transparent materials, this ingratiating figure shows the technical assurance of a virtuoso of vivid contemporary portraits.

WALDO PEIRCE.—Maine Swimming Hole. Private Collection.

Teaming with exuberant life, Peirce's scenes harmonize the human figure with its natural background. His color is high, his brushwork loose and easy in the manner of the Impressionists.

cal bent lends his figures a detached, doll-like look. Du Bois' excellent portraits are free of the mannerisms of his other works. Even to-day, when it comes to portraits, the majority of sitters choose an artist who can be counted on to depict the outer shape rather than the inner truth. Some modern Americans can do both. Take Charles Brackman. His technique is academic, his figures, bathed in silvery space, arrested in time, nevertheless have a strength of characterization which makes them live, especially his portraits of men. A more dashing interpretation is Eugene Speicher's, intent on the vribant aspects of color, texture and personality. A figure painter who has achieved something of Renoir's earthy naturalness is Waldo

THOMAS HART BENTON.—First Crop. New York,
Collection International Business Machines Corp.

*Leading figure in America's first genuine regional school, Benton convention-
alizes local material, and is at his best in murals, in which medium he has completed some of the country's most important commissions.*

Peirce. Like the Frenchman, he has found his best subjects near at hand
in his own exuberant family.

In 1920 a young Iowan called Grant Wood went to Europe to absorb
art at its fountain-head. After his fourth trip abroad he came to the con-
clusion that the material he had seen while milking cows and mowing
lawns in Cedar Rapids, Iowa, was worth more than all the apples and
checked tablecloths of the Left Bank. A remarkable natural draftsman,
he renders small-town Midwest types with fanatical fidelity, landscapes in
a crisp, toy-like idiom. His influence on American art was enormous.

Two others, also refugees from Paris bohemianism, crystallised in paint

REGINALD MARSH.—Martial Spirit. Private Collection.

The most blatant or commercial aspects of American life are invested with authentic vitality by Marsh, who sees in city crowds a continuous motif or frieze related to Baroque decorative forms.

CHARLES E. BURCHFIELD.—The Great Elm.   Pittsburgh, Carnegie Institute.

Early protagonist of the American Scene, Burchfield developed an individual style in schematizing nature.   His most successful medium is watercolor which he puts to new uses, expanding a technique of the nineteenth century to meet the demands of the twentieth.

this Walt Whitmanesque vision of America.   John Steuart Curry, born in Kansas, did farm chores as a boy, grew up to interpret American folk tales in a tumultuous style.   Thomas Benton, born in Missouri, once worked as a stevedore, became the Midwest's best salesmen of the back-to-the-land idea.   Missouri's mules, cornstalks, meeting-houses he handles with Breughel-like, anecdotal animation.   Where Curry is chaotic, finds the vision too big, Benton is tight, self-conscious, mannered.   Artistically, neither was Wood's equal, yet each played his part in popularising the American Scene—a designation which soon came to rate capital letters.

The list of artists which can be appended here is hard to limit, the following being only a cross-section.   At his head stands Reginald Marsh, recorder of the gaudy jungles under the El, the teaming, steaming crowds of Coney Island.   Better draftsman than painter, he made an extensive study of 18th century drawing methods, successfully emulating their vaporous washes and characterful line in a rare combination of veracity and

GRANT WOOD.—Spring in the Country.   Terre-Haute,
The Swope Art Gallery.

*Originator of the American Scene movement, Wood simplified and re-inter-
preted what he saw around him in his native Iowa.   Although his idiom was
widely imitated, no artist has approached his sincerity of expression.*

EDWARD HOPPER.—Sunday on Main Street. Washington, D. C.,
Phillips Memorial Gallery.

*The deathly stillness which pervades this picture is the typical atmosphere of
Hopper's work. In cool, technically competent detachment, he presides over
the haunting melancholy of his pictures.*

grace. Born in Russia, the Soyer Raphael, Isaacs and Moses, render one
of the more convincing accounts of New York, especially of the immigrant
element to which they themselves belong. The forlorn uncertainty of
these new Americans in enhanced by their background of characterless
hallways and impersonal furnished rooms. Charles Burchfield was a pioneer in painting a new favorite type of Americana: the "ghost houses"
built by pretentious Victorians. Edward Hopper envelops deserted streets
and glaring theater lobbies alike in a curious remoteness—a sense of

ISAAC SOYER.—Office Girls.   New York, Collection Pepsi-Cola.

No scene is too mundane, no incident too petty to solicit Soyer's interest. Comparable to newspaper reporting, veracious but compassionate, it lends importance to the lives of anonymous passers-by.

WILLIAM GROPPER.—Joe Magarac. Gimbel Pennsylvania Art Collection.

A tireless fighter for liberal causes, Gropper has kept his art down to a stark minimum in line, color and finish. Many of his political satires bite deep in their indictment of official justice.

ROBERT GWATHMEY.—Hoeing. Pittsburg, Carnegie Institute.

Eloquent crusader for social equality, Gwathmey combines poster-like starkness with linear subtleties, unexpected tonal dissonances and a palette of unexcelled freshness and brilliance.

the strange in the very element that is most familiar—which foreshadows the Magic Realists.

Once we start enumerating American Scene painters, it is hard to stop. The land is full of canvases depicting gasoline stations or cityscapes crisscrossed by electric power lines. There are pictures of dingy suburbs under rutted, gutted snow; of Kansas wheatfields and cactus-dotted Western droughtscapes; of dumps haunted by the ghosts of 1920 Ford sedans and turreted mansarded architectural relics.

In 1933 the second depression hit rock bottom. By 1935 one of the many insoluble problems undertaken by the Government concerned the unemployed artist. Hailed as the instrument of Utopia, derogated as the agent of subversive New Deal politics, the PWA (later WPA) in the long run justified the inevitable incompetents and chiselers on its payroll by producing some very affirmative results. Among others, it gave a start to many talented socially-conscious young artists who represent the typical

JACOB LAWRENCE.—Tombstones. New York, Whitney Museum of
American Art.

*One of a long series which celebrates Negro life both in the city and in migration,
this picture has typical balance and color richness. Lawrence is all the more
eloquent for being a quiet propagandist.*

EUGENE BERMAN.—Napolitana. Pennsylvania, Collection
Mr. and Mrs. Henry Clifford, Radnor.

*Leading Neo-Romantic, Berman influenced Americans, encouraging a distinct
native trend toward Surrealism. With its haunting sense of death and decay,
his work epitomizes the spirit of moral lassitude between wars.*

WERNER DREWES.—Still-life. New York, Collection International Business Machines Corp.

Early emmisary to America from Germany's Bauhaus, Drewes' forms, half organic, half mechanical, fitted life in the New World, and stimulated American abstractionists to develop their own solutions.

SALVADOR DALI.—Paranoiac Astral Image. Hartford, Connectient,
Wadsworth Atheneum.

*Technical brilliance, with Dali, lends conviction to extravagant subject matter
by clothing the unexpected in the common light of day. His earlier pictures,
such as this, have a deeply haunting quality.*

voice of the mid-1930's. In those days, left-right battles were an open issue.
Painter-propagandists often became so excited over them that zeal outstripped technical means. To-day the pamphleteers have dropped out of
the picture; those with a genuine artistic message have become part of
U.S. art. Veteran of the latter is William Gropper, master of scathing
denunciation who makes no secret of his debt to Daumier, complete with
law courts, declamatory diagonals and an austere sense of black and white.
Philip Evergood's weapon is satire, sometimes subtle, sometimes overdone,
at its best highly eloquent. Robert Gwathmey, over and above his drama-
tization of the plight of sharecroppers black and white, is a natural com-
poser interms of line and color. The most desperate theme is presented
in a palette of coral-to-magenta pinks, of acid greens and sulphur yellows,
of chocolate browns and grey. Jacob Lawrence, a Negro painter who has

MARCEL VERTÈS.—Woman at the Window. New York, Private Collection.

A light, frothy touch in Vertès' art is apt to distract attention from the underlying quality of his work, which includes a poignant gift for caricature and a fleeting, evocative sense of beauty.

LYONEL FEININGER.—Fisher Off the Coast. Detroit, Michigan,
Newbury Collection.

*The infinitely distant, delicate gradations of this artist's work are almost
Oriental in their understatement. Ships at sea are a subject peculiarly suited
to the prismatic transparencies of his work.*

depicted with quiet forcefulness the migrations of his people, their life in
segregated city areas, their philosophic acceptance of what seem incurable
conditions, also achieves a high degree of artistic as well as social significance.
Ben Shahn, with his subtle dislocations, his occasional wild excursions into
fantasy or humor, is harder to classify. Often he paints without relief or
roundness or tonal gradations, one bright color singing stridently out of key.
But whether his subject is a sculpture gallery or children swinging wildly
among the ruins of a bombed city, the impact is always there.

Inevitable as the motion of a pendulum, America was destined to swing
back into the sphere of Europe. No matter how valid, the chauvinistic
school inevitably grew monotonous. Americans love change for its own
sake. So when the first wave of political émigrés from Europe arrived in
the late 1930's, these men promptly got one-man shows and before long
were being imitated. War and the country's enlarging political horizons
completed the transformation. In time, many of these foreign talents became American citizens, guaranteeing the permanent transplantation of
ideas from Old World to New.

Three names that stand out are Salvador Dali, Eugene Berman and Pavel

PAVEL TCHELITCHEW.—Fallen Rider. New Jersey.
CollectionMrs. Lloyd Wescott.

*A leading Neo-Romantic in the Paris of the 1920's, Tchelitchew subsequently
developed the enigmatical aspects of form into multiple images of amazing
fantasy. He has also designed brilliant stage sets.*

Tchelitchew. Dali, an unexcelled exhibitionist who conducted his own
under-water peep-show at the World's Fair, aroused both indignation at
his escapades and envy at his accomplishments. His biggest influence
today can be traced in advertising art, which has capitalized on his technique of incongruities and surprises. Both leaders of the Neo-Romantic
movement, Berman and Tchelitchew, opened up a new, imaginative vista
to Americans, who were quick to sense the compulsion of the former's
tatters and ruins, the vision of the latter's double images. Marcel Vertès,
with his background of stage designer and caricaturist, set a new standard
in fashion drawing. Piet Mondrian, the great constructivist, gave confidence to America's rising school of Abstractionists, influenced everything
from page layout to the design of linoleum, as did exponents of the Bau-

DIEGO RIVERA.—The Offering. New York, Museum of Modern Art.

The first of the Mexicans to realize the inexhaustible richness of his native subject matter, Rivera is a brilliant technician, as effective in a study such as this as in a vast mural.

HECTOR POLEO.—The Andean Family. New York,
Collection International Business Machines Corp.

*Of humble origins, with enormous talent to replace education, the young
Venezuelan Poleo has created moving and accomplished canvases of great artistic integrity.   His color recalls Italian primitives.*

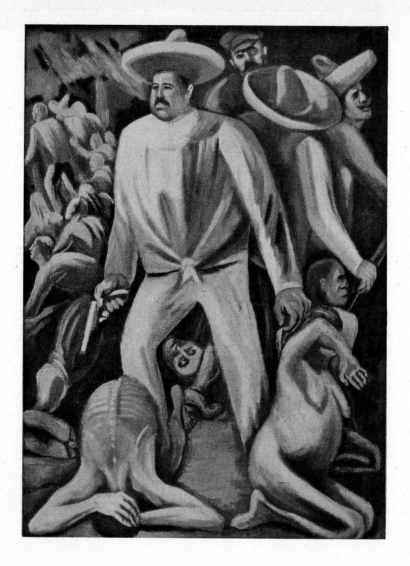

JOSE CLEMENTE OROZCO.—Pancho Villa. New York, Private Collection.

Most declamatory of Mexican artistic leaders, this painter carried on the fight against capitalist oppression with dynamic violence. His murals in public building rank second only to those of Rivera.

RUFINO TAMAYO.—Watermelons.   Private Collection.

A ferocious primitivism in Tamayo's work is the echo of his Aztec ancestry. Alternately laden with earth tones or flamboyant with magentas, pinks and greens, his color is a part of modern Mexico.

haus æsthetic, notably Werner Drewes. Two German painters gave further dimension to America's artistic outlook, Lyonel Feininger as the exponent of a crystalline, mystic latter-day Cubism; and Max Beckmann who represents the German Expressionist school with a power and eloquence which is bound to bear fruit.

Of the Latin-American countries, Mexico is the one which has made a real contribution to the artistic scene in the United States. Early in the 1920's there were much-discussed showings of Mexican art. Personalities, such as Rivera and Orozco visited the country to leave behind them indestructible arguments in the form of murals. The excitement of Mexico's artistic revolution (which succeeded the political one by about ten years) has never entirely been forgotten.

The year 1921 plays a crucial part in this movement as it saw the founding of the Mexican school which began as a technique and ended as a new æsthetic. Several years before, Diego Rivera had returned from Paris, where he had associated with Picasso, and from Italy, where he had filled notebooks with classical drawings. He soon became the leading figure in his country's artistic rebirth. In 1920 President Obregon put art patronage on a government basis by appointing Vasconcelos Minister of Education. The latter offered to Mexico's artists that greatest of gifts: unlimited wall space upon which to express their doctrines. In the courtyards, stairways and halls of public buildings, the country's best artists left their political sermons in permanent form.

Diego Rivera represents not only the intellectual side of the movement, but the most technically varied contribution. He has created superb murals (the finest, artistically, in Mexico, the most controversial in the United States); line drawings that rival Picasso's; and endless studies in oil, sanguine, watercolor. All have not only technical proficiency but the gift of utter naturalness applied to one of the freshest and most eminently paintable subjects: the native life and color of Mexico.

Jose Clemente Orozco belonged in the early days to what was called the "Jungle Group" of propagandizing young enthusiasts, to which Siqueiros also belonged. Even the Mexicans themselves find the subjects of his murals enigmatical, but no one will deny their power. Nudes which look like "skeletons robed in flesh," cruel caricatures and chains form a stock part of his artistic language. Like the Italian Mannerists, Orozco prefers the dramatic diagonal. His color is often limited to black, white, a cold pitiless grey and a flashing metallic red.

David Alfaro Siqueiros likes to convey his enormous message in the form of super-expressive, out-size heads whose thick Duco surface is carried to a point of sculptural relief thanks to the use of a spray gun. As with most Mexican artists, for whom the *calavera* or animated skeleton has long been

CANDIDO PORTINARI.—Woman and Children. New York,
Collection International Business Machines Corp.

*Brazil's leading painter was once a photographic portraitist and, following
that, an epic muralist. To-day, in a local idiom, he has recaptured some of
the dynamism of the European Expressionists.*

JACKSON POLLOCK.—Shadows.   Private Collection.

Amorphic form, pioneered by Miro and Arp, have been developed still further in America by certain young artists who have made of them a tapestry as diversified in its interest as it is plastic in its rich paint surfaces.

ALBERT PINKHAM RYDER.—Siegfried and the Rhine Maidens.
Washington, D. C., National Gallery of Art.

*The immediate father of modern Romanticism, Ryder occasionally borrowed
nineteenth-century narrative devices, as here, at other times developed his own
original poetry built on the theme of moody, moonlit scenes.*

a familiar effigy, the sense of death is frequently present in his works.
Carlos Merida, a Guatemalan who lived in Mexico, was influenced both by
the shapes of Pre-Columbian art and by the Paris idiom. His rhyming
outlines have the intuitive rightness of the born Abstractionist. Typifying

EILSHEMIUS.—Cabs for Hire.   Washington, D. C., Phillips Memorial Gallery.
Forgotten artist in his time, Eilshemius enjoyed belated success along with the revival of Romanticism.   Appreciated at last were his poetic lyricism, his color, the innocent, pastoral loveliness of his subjects.

the dramatic Aztec strain in Mexican art is Rufino Tamayo whose ferocious bestiary and aboriginal humans are translated into art thanks to a superb color sense.   He represents the revolution's ultimate negation of Spanish colonial influence.

One other Latin-American looms equally important alongside the Mexicans. This is Candido Portinari, leading modern painter of Brazil, an artist of enormous range and capacity.   Portinari's portraits are of a smooth, flawless verisimilitude.   His big decorative works (such as *Coffee*, which won honorable mention at the 1935 Carnegie International) have as much sweep as Mexican murals.   Looser and freer are a type of fantasy built around a central scarecrow-like construction.   The interest here is the play between

WILLIAM THON.—Aunt Thankful's Farm.   Coll. Dr. and Mrs. R. C. Brown.

Evocative, emotional, Thon has painted the stormy sea, the poetry of winter and, of late, while on a trip to Europe, the classic Mediterranean sites of Romanticism, but with a difference.

light and dark, the flicker of white against rich handsome browns, deep blues and maroons.

In a wholly different vein is the work of the self-taught Venezuelan Hector Poleo, whose exact, crystal-clear scenes of his arid homeland have surreal overtones, whose portraits and figure paintings recall the mournful mysticism of fifteenth century Italian art.   Cuba is represented by Mariano Carreño.   Although his early figure pieces were influenced by the "classic" period Picassos, these have been succeeded by more richly imaginative semi-abstractions built around the African imagery of West Indian art.

Abstraction is a mode basically suited to Americans.   Starting with Stuart Davis, who backed the Armory Show and made contact with theories being developed by Picasso, Gris, Braque, it has prospered increasingly. To-day its battles are over.   The banding together of the American Abstract Artists in 1938 rounded up diverse talents which had hitherto been able to show only within local coteries or not at all.   There were two main camps. The Museum of Living Art Group, founded in 1927 by A. E. Gallatin (himself a painter of handsome, orderly compositions) included George L. K. Morris,

WALTER STUEMPFIG.—Street Music.   Art Association of Indianapolis.

There is an almost Surreal feeling to many of Stuempfig's paintings. Under his brush, a purely American subject seems like a place glimpsed before, apprehended by generations of Romantic artists.

JOHN CARROLL.—Spring Bonnet.   Private Collection.

*From the type of the women he chooses as models to his muted palette of greys,
rose and silver with deep charcoal shadows, Carroll acknowledges himself
to be a confirmed Romantic.*

Philip Guston.—Night Children. New York, Midtown Galleries.

The world's topsy-turvy is interpreted in the work of Guston who likes to translate its and his own conflicts in the form of a masquerade whose protagonists are children too young to understand.

who made interesting use of American Indian material in energetic, stark abstractions.

Rival patron of the early days of American abstraction was the Museum of Non-Objective Art, where painters such as the talented Irene Rice-Peireira got her start. To-day Miss Rice-Pereira has made the outstanding technical advance in the abstract field, creating three-dimensional effects with corrugated glass and polaroid.

Within the last five years another a new type of abstraction has appeared, widely orchestrated, comparable to an endless running tapestry of which the framed portion which the painter has captured on canvas represents but a fragment. Jackson Pollock and William Baziotes are leading exponents of this school where amorphic forms suggest the new world of science under the microscope.

DARREL AUSTIN.—The Vixen. Boston, Mass., Museum of Fine Arts.

Out of strange pictures of swamps and ghostly beasts, Austin achieved a quick rise to fame. His paint texture is rich and varied and lends a great interest to a predominant palette of watery greens, blues and blacks.

JULIO DE DIEGO.—International Poker Players.   New York,
Associated American Artists.

*The many styles which this artist has pursued makes it impossible to classify
his work.   In all, however, he remains an inexhaustible fantasist with a special
gift for presenting abstract ideas in precise visual terms.*

HORACE PIPPIN.—After Supper, West Chester.   Private Collection.

The innocent vision of this artist, coupled with extraordinary sensitiveness both as to color and composition, give his work rare distinction.   Self-taught, Pippin instinctively knew the aesthetic rules that other artists often never acquire.

Ever since the Hudson River painters, the Romantic school has provided contrapuntal relief to the factual element in American painting.   At the beginning of the century, it found its greatest exponent in William Ryder, whose visionary, moonlit fantasies of stormy seas and scudding clouds rank with the literary accomplishments of Edgar Allen Poe.   By contrast, his contemporary Louis Eilshemius, despite the rather lumbering quality of his human figures, painted landscapes of an almost Arcadian glow and innocence.   Of the two, Ryder has been the dominant influence.   A number of painters today work in his idiom and palette, most notably Henry

ANDREW WYETH.—Self-Portrait. New York, National Academy of Design.

A young artist of great promise, member of a painting clan, Wyeth introduces into his self-portrait the same quiet, enigmatical quality that pervades his landscapes and scenes of country life.

Mattson, of the tossing, green-black marines, and William Thon, who makes haunting poetry out of the devastation of winter. John Carroll dreams of wraith-like women dappled by shadow and moonlight; Walter Stuempfig lifts native material out of the American Scene rut, thanks to an Italianate sense of style. Here too, Kuniyoshi ranks high. From his neat, witty early paintings, he developed a loose, luminous technique in silvery greys to describe some of the most truly Romantic figure pieces in American painting.

Although Surrealism in the Dali idiom has become too much associated

HENRY KOERNER.—Vanity Fair. New York, Whitney Museum
of American Art.

*The spectacular rise of Koerner, which began with a Berlin exhibit during
his service with the American Army, is justified by his sure technique, the
urgent and highly provocative nature of his subjects.*

with advertising to tempt many serious artists, a fantastic strain was
undoubtedly released by the Surrealist's uninhibited choice of subject
matter. In 1942 an exhibition of Americans at the Museum of Modern
Art brought two of these unexpected talents to light: Morris Graves and
Darrel Austin, both of the Northwest. Graves, in his early manner,
handled his line as if it were an incantation, spun ectoplasmic birds' nests,
amplified these brilliant scribblings until they became the whole subject

PAUL CADMUS.—The Shower. New York, Collection A. B. Campbell.
Alternately satirical and surreal, Cadmus describes his subjects in a close-focus technique that brooks no denial. Slow and deliberate, his pencil drawings are prized collectors' items.

of the picture. Austin painted weird animals—a fox, a bull, a lioness, later puckish humans—distorted them to the limits of his expressive purpose, set them in a landscape of phosphorescent marshland. Philip Guston, with his symbolism of masks and upsidedown figures superimposed in a kind

STEPHEN GREENE.—Burial. New York, Whitney Museum of American Art.

Most compelling of the new-generation artists thanks to the burden of personal responsability which his pictures imply, Greene's art is not without hope, as expressed in his radiant color and vibrant paint quality.

of wild carnival, suggests the dislocations of modern life. Spanishborn Julio de Diego is brilliant both as a painter and imagist; Loren MacIver's wispy, flickering impressions are lit by a delicate poetry.

Genuine primitivism is rare in the country of the movies and the corner drugstore. A few, however, have retained the innocent eye in the 20th century (there were plenty in the 19th and earlier). Outstanding was a Pittsburg paver and house painter called John Kane, who brought the mystical intensity of a deeply religious mind to his work. The Negro artist Horace Pippin ranks alonside European primitives like Rousseau the Douanier, Bombois and Peyronnet for the innate rightness of his style, plus a great color sense.

In 1943 the Museum of Modern Art held an exhibition which was destined to have a long-range effect on American painting. Under the title "Realists and Magic Realists," it rounded up and gave standing to a type of work which was being produced spontaneously in different parts of the country. Regarded superficially, the common element among these pictures was a technical one: a minutious exactitude of rendition. But upon second glance, it was obvious that the artists shared something more than good eyesight and a steady brush. The best of them had the ability to make their subject, in its very reality, seem strange. The aim of many Surrealists, including Dali, this technique was stripped of incongruous subject matter and obvious surprises. Take, for example, Andrew Wyeth. Over and again the observer searches his low-keyed, beautifully-painted farm scenes for some clew to the mystery he senses there—in the frozen grass, the dead bird, the pushing bramble, the cracked plaster. Charles Rain's small, perfect canvasses give a fourth-dimensional quality to a berry, a drop of dew on a leaf, which makes his occasional excursion into Surrealism seem supererogatory. In figure pieces, the Magic Realist technique has been adopted by two trenchant satirists. Paul Cadmus, as one of our best draftsmen, uses this skill to show up his contemporary man (a creature whom he obviously does not admire). The weaknesses of lustful sailors, maudlin Babbits, rapacious tarts are deeply etched in the lines of their faces. Henry Kœrner satirizes more subtly, with less condemnation. His gnomish figures, against war-shattered backgrounds, are curiously moving because he neither rejects nor criticises them. A couple sitting in a derelict car which has come to a permanent standstill in a vacant lot, overdressed tourists feeding pigeons surrounded by apathetic poverty—all these rendered in crystal clear, meticulous detail—rank as milestones in American art.

For his part, Stephen Greene adopted the Magic Realist technique because he wanted to "paint tragedy with as much beauty as possible." His first subjects were cripples, who seemed less relics of the last war than a forecast of coming disaster. Later he transferred this intense sense of pity to semi-religious themes. With no literal representation, a complex of ladders and figures by Greene gives the feeling of a Descent from the Cross. He and Koerner epitomize the serious outlook of a certain number of young artists who sense the responsibility of their times.

Thus from the decorative, the grandiose and the escapist which prevailed at the beginnings of this century, art has come to grips with life in all its atomic-age strangeness. These last-mentioned painters are as faithful exponents of the realism of their day as were their earlier, more comprehensible ancestors.

BIBLIOGRAPHY

FRENCH PAINTING IN THE 19th CENTURY

L. HAUTECŒUR.—Rome et la Renaissance, de l'Antiquité à la fin du xviiie siècle; Paris, 1912.

L. HAUTECŒUR.—Grands Artistes; Paris, 1914.

P. DE NOLHAC.—Fragonard; new ed., 1931.

CH. BLANC.—Histoire des peintres français au xixe siècle; Paris, 1845.

BAUDELAIRE.—L'Art romantique. Curiosités esthétiques; Paris, 1868

HUYSMANS.—L'Art moderne; Paris, 1883.

ROSENBERG.—Geschichte der französischen Kunst; 1884.

L. HAUTECŒUR.—David; 1949.

L. REAU.—L'Art romantique; 1930.

R. ESCHOLIER.—E. Delacroix, peintre, graveur, écrivain (3 vol.); 1926-1929

P. DORBEC.—L'Art du paysage en France de la fin du xviiie siècle au second Empire; 1925.

J. W. MOLLET.—The Painters of Barbizon (2 vol.); London, 1890.

GERMAIN BAZIN.—Corot, 1942.

ARSENE ALEXANDRE.—Honoré Daumier, l'homme et son œuvre; Paris, 1888.

MOREAU-NELATON.—Millet raconté par lui-même (3 vol.); 1932.

C. MAUCLAIR.—Les Grands Peintres français de 1830 à nos jours; London, 1903.

C. MAUCLAIR.—L'Impressionnisme; Paris, 1903.

DURET.—Histoire des peintres impressionnistes; Paris, new ed., 1922.

ÉLIE FAURE.—Histoire de l'Art (4 vol.); Paris, 1911 and foll.

FOCILLON.—La Peinture du xixe et du xxe siècle. Manuels d'histoire de l'art; Paris, 1927-1928.

GILLET.—Histoire des Arts (Histoire de la Nation française, de Hanotaux); Paris, 1924.

G. POULAIN.—Bazille et ses amis; Paris, 1932.

CH. TERRASSE.—Pierre Bonnard; Paris, 1927.

W. H. WRIGHT.—Modern Painting; New York, 1915.

B. DORIVAL.—Les Étapes de la peinture française contemporaine; Paris, 1945.

GERMAIN BAZIN.—L'Époque impressionniste; Paris, 1947.

E. A. JEWELL.—Cézanne; New York, 1944.

J. LASSAIGNE.—Degas; Paris, 1948.

J. REWALD.—Gauguin; Paris and London, 1949.

P. SIGNAC.—Jongkind; Paris, 1927.

E. ZOLA.—Manet, étude biographique et critique; Paris, 1867.

G. GEOFFROY.—Claude Monet, sa vie, son temps, son œuvre; Paris, 1922.

CL. ROGER-MARX.—Redon; Paris, 1925.

GERMAIN BAZIN.—Renoir; Geneva, 1947.

P. JAMOT.—G.B.A. nov.-déc.;Paris, 1923.

J. REWALD.—Seurat; New York, 1943, and Paris, 1947.

H. HELLMAIER.—Die Kunst für Alle; 1930-1931.

J. LASSAIGNE.—Toulouse-Lautrec; Paris, 1939.

L. VENTRI.—Les Arts plastiques; Bruxelles, 1947.

M. FLORISOONE.—V. Van Gogh; Paris, 1937.

MAURICE RAYNAL.—De Baudelaire à Bonnard; Geneva, 1949.

P. G. HAMERTON.—Contemporary French Painters; London, 1868.

A. HOEBER.—The Barbizon Painters; New York, 1915.

S. ROCHEBLAVE.—La Peinture française au xixᵉ siècle; Paris, 1936.

JEWELL and CRANE.—French Impressionists; New York, 1944.

ENGLISH PAINTING IN THE 19th CENTURY

W. KNIGHT.—Nineteenth Century Artists English and French; 1910.

W. C. MONKHOUSE.—British Contemporary Artists; New York, 1899.

W. T. WHITLEY.—Art in England, 1800-1820 and 1821-1837 (2 vol.); London, 1928 and 1930.

W. H. HUNT.—Pre-Raphaelitism and the Pre-Raphaelite Brotherhood (2 vol.); New York, 1914.

A. DUBUISSON.—Richard Parkes Bonington; 1924.

M. BELL.—Sir Edward Burne-Jones; 1898.

F. M. HUEFFER.—Ford Madox Brown; 1896.

C. J. HOLMES.—Constable; 1902.

S. D. KITSON.—The Life of John Sell Cotman; 1937.

LORD R. GOWER.—Sir Thomas Lawrence; 1900.

J. G. MILLAIS.—Life of Sir J. E. Millais; 1901.

SIR J. CAW.—Portraits of Sir Henry Raeburn; 1909.

H. C. MARILLIER.—Dante Gabriel Rossetti; 1901.

C. MAUCLAIR.—Turner; Paris, 1939.

M. S. WATTS.—George Frederick Watts; 1912.

CENTRAL EUROPEAN PAINTING IN THE 19th CENTURY

C. GURLITT.—Deutsche Kunst des XIX. Jahrh; 1907.

LUDWIG JUSTI.—Deutsche Malkunst des XIX. Jahrh; 1921.

W. R. DEUSCH.—Malerai der deutschen Romantiker; 1937.

U. CHRISTOFFEL.—Die romantische Zeichnung, 1920.

P. F. SCHMIDT.—Deutsche Malerei um 1880 : I. Landschaftsmalerei, 1922. II. Bildnis and Komposition, 1928.

THIEME und BECKER.—Allgemeines Lexikon der bildenden Künstler; 1931.

ANDREAS AUBERT.—Runge und die Romantik; 1909.

HERBERT EINEM.—Caspar David Friedrich; 1938.

C. G. HEISE.—Overbeck und sein Kreis; 1928.

J. MEIER-GRAEFE.—Der junge Menzel; 1914.

H. A. SCHMIDT.—Arnold Böcklin; 1922.

GUSTAV PAULI.—Max Liebermann; 1911.

KARL VOLL.—Max Slevogt; 1912.

H. MUHLESTEIN.—Ferdinand Hodler; 1914.

AMERICAN PAINTING IN THE 19th CENTURY

FREDERICK A. SWEET.—The Hudson River School; Chicago, Catalogue to exhibition organized by the Chicago Art Institute and the Whitney Museum of American Art, 1943.

SAMULE ISHAM.—History of American Painting; New York, 1936.

HOLGER CAHILL and ALFRED BARR Jr.—Art in America; New York, 1935.

J. W. McSPADDEN.—Famous Painters of America; New York, 1907.

G. W. SHELDON.—American Painters; with examples of their work; London, 1879.

HOMER ST. GAUDENS.—Survey of American Painting. Pittsburg, Carnegie Institute Department of Fine Arts. Catalogue to the Carnegie exhibition, 1940.

FRANK JEWETT MATHER.—Estimates in Art; New York, 1931.

SAMUEL M. KOOTZ.—Modern American Painters; Norwood, Mass., 1930.

CLARA ERSKINE CLEMENT and LAURENCE HUTTON.—Artiste of the Nineteenth Century and their Works; Boston, 1879.

WILLIAM HOWE DOWNES.—Twelve Great Artists; Boston, 1900.

FREDERICK FAIRCHILD SHERMAN.—Landscape and Figure Painting; New York, 1917.

EUROPEAN PAINTING IN THE 20th CENTURY

H. FOCILLON.—La Peinture au XIXe et au XXe siècle; 1928.

MAURICE RAYNAL.—Peintres du XXe siècle; Genève, 1948.

F. AHLERS-HESTERMANN.—Stilwende, Aufbruch der Jugend um 1900; 1941.

MAX SAUERLANDT.—Die Kunst der letzten dreissig Jahre 1935.

Collection.—Junge Kunst (Monographies of Artists); Leipzig, 1921.

PAUL WESTHEIM.—Oskar Kokoschka; 1918.

MATEJCEK.—L'Art tchèque contemporain.

BELA LAZAR.—Le Livre du Musée Ernst; Budapest, 1923.

CARL LAMM.—Nordisk Kunst; Stockholm, 1926.

K. UMANSKIJ.—Neue Kunst in Russland; 1928.

PAUL COLIN.—La Peinture belge depuis 1830.

M. EISLER.—Modern Dutch portrait painting; 1911.

G. VIDALENC.—L'Art norvégien contemporain; Paris, 1921.

KANDINSKY and FRANZ MARC.—Der Blaue Reiter; Munich, 1912.

WILLY HANSENSTEIN.—Die bildende Kunst der Gegenwart; Munich, 1914.

K. EDSCHMIED.—Ueber den Expressionismus; Berlin, 1918.

F. ROH.—Nachexpressionismus, Magischer Realismus, Probleme der neuesten europäischen Malerei; Leipzig, 1925.

H. KLUMPF.—Abstraktion in der Malerei: Kandinsky, Feininger, Klee; Berlin, 1931.

WITH.—Marc Chagall; 1920.

L. ZAHN.—Paul Klee; 1920.

REIFFENBERG and HAUSENSTEIN.—Max Beckmann; 1949.

OTTO DIX.—Der Krieg; 1946.

H. BUNNEMANN.—Franz Marc; 1948.

R. H. WILENSKI.—Modern Movement in Art; New York, 1927.

R. H. WILENSKI.—Modern French Painters; New York, 1940.

ALFRED H. BARR Jr.—Cubism and Abstract Art; New York, 1936.

ALFRED H. BARR Jr.—Fantastic Art, Dada, Surrealism; New York, 1936.

HERBERT READ.—Art Now; New York, 1934.

MAURICE REYNAL.—Modern French Painters; New York, 1928; London, 1929.

JAMES THRALL SOBY.—After Picasso; New York, 1935.

A. GLEIZES and J. METZINGER.—Cubism; London, 1913.

J. GORDON.—Modern French Painters; New York, 1923; London, 1926.

ANDRÉ MICHEL (Publié sous la direction de).—Histoire de l'Art, t. VIII.

L. REAU.—La Peinture française de 1848 à nos jours; Paris, 1926.

L. HAUTECŒUR.—Réflexions sur la peinture d'aujourd'hui; *Revue de Paris*, 1927.

RAYMOND ESCHOLIER.—La Peinture française au xxe siècle; Paris, 1937.

J. COCTEAU.—Picasso; Paris, 1923.

CHARENSOL.—Rouault; Paris, Chroniques du Jour.

MAITRES POPULAIRES DE LA RÉALITÉ.—Catalogue de l'Exposition organisée par le Musée de Grenoble; Paris, 1937.

JEAN CASSOU.—Picasso; Paris, 1939.

RENÉ HUYGHE.—Les Contemporains; Paris, 1949.

CH. TERRASSE.—La Peinture française au xxe siècle; Paris, 1939.

J. LASSAIGNE.—Cent chefs-d'œuvre de l'École de Paris; Paris, 1947.

VENTURI.—La Peinture contemporaine; Milan, 1948.

CLIVE BELL.—Victor Pasmore. Modern Painters Series; London, 1949.

JOHN BETJEMAN.—John Piper. Modern Painters Series; London, 1948.

ROBIN IRONSIDE.—Painting since 1939. Art in Britain Series; London, 1948.

ROBIN IRONSIDE.—David Jones. Modern Painters Series; London, 1949.

RAYMOND MORTIMER.—Duncan Grant. Modern Painters Series; London, 1948.

ERIC NEWTON.—British Painting. British Life and Thought Series; London, 1948.

ERIC NEWTON.—Stanley Spencer. Modern Painters Series; London, 1949.

HERBERT READ.—Art Now; 1948.

HERBERT READ.—Ben Nicholson; London, 1948.

JOHN ROTHENSTEIN.—Introduction to English Painting; London, 1949.

JOHN RUSSELL.—From Sickert to 1948; London, 1949.

AMERICAN PAINTING IN THE 20th CENTURY

MUSEUM OF MODERN ART.—Art in our Time; New York, Museum of Modern Art, 1939.

J. WALKER.—Great American Paintings from Smibert to Bellows; New York, 1944.

R. H. WILENSKI.—Modern Movement in Art; New York, 1927.

FORBES WATSON.—American Painting Today; New York, 1939.

PEYTON BOSWELL, Jr.—Modern American Painting; New York, 1940.

SHELDON CHENEY.—The Story of Modern Art; New York, 1941.

MARCHAL E. LANDGREN.—Years of Art; New York, 1940.

FROST and CRANE.—Contemporary Art; New York, 1942.

A. CASO, M. TOUSSAINT and M. COVARRUBIAS.—Twenty Centuries of Mexican Art. New York, Museum of Modern Art, 1940.

BIOGRAPHIES

ALLSTON, Washington. American School. 1779-1843. (Pages: 141, 142, 149). — Born in South Carolina, he grew up in Rhode Island, graduated from Harvard and eventually joined Benjamin West's studio in London. There followed years in Paris and Rome and an extended stay in England. In 1818, he opened a studio in Boston which, as he was a poet and author as well as a painter, became a center of cultural life. He is prized today as America's earliest outstanding Romantic.

ALMA-TADEMA, Sir Lawrence. English School. 1836-1912. (Page: 100).— The son of a notary, he intended to be a doctor and did not take up painting until 1852, when he entered the Academy of Antwerp. Naturalized a British subject, he settled in London in 1873. His work was inspired by his studies of Egyptian archeology and Greco-Roman art. He was elected a member of the Royal Academy in 1879 and knighted in 1905.

AMIET, Cuno. Swiss School. 1868. (Page: 249.)—Born March 28, 1868, at Soleure (Switzerland). He received his artistic training in Switzerland, Munich and Paris. Having participated in the foundation of the "Brücke," he always retained a free and robust craftsmanship.

AUBERJONOIS, René. School of Paris. 1872. (Page: 249.)—Born August 18, 1872, at Yverdon (Switzerland). Studied in London as well as in Paris where he later spent a great deal of time, always keeping in close contact with French painting.

AUSTIN, Darrel. American School. 1907. (Pages: 330, 331.)—Born Raymond, Washington, he studied at the University of Oregon (where he painted murals), Columbia University and Notre Dame. His first one-man show was held in 1938, in California. His work is included in the Metropolitan Museum of Art; the Museum of Modern Art; the William Rockhill Nelson Gallery, Kansas City; the museums of Boston, Detroit, Philadelphia and others.

AVERY, Milton. American School. 1893. (Pages: 297, 300.)—Born Altmar, N. Y., studied Connecticut League of Art Students and at Hartford Art Society, supporting himself by night-time factory work. 1926, moved to New York, since then has exhibited widely and successfully, holds Connecticut League Atheneum Prize, Third Logan Prize, First Prize at the Baltimore Annual Watercolor Show.

B

BAZILLE, Jean-Frédéric. French School. 1841-1870. (Pages: 41, 42, 51.)— A pupil of Gleyre, he exhibited at the Salon in 1866. He was a friend of Monet, Renoir and Sisley. He died very young, killed in the battle of Beaune-la-Rolande.

BAZIOTES, William. American School. 1912. (Page: 327.)—Born in Pittsburg, Baziotes studied at the National Academy of Design in New York. In 1947, his work took first prize in a Chicago Art Institute exhibit of abstract and surrealist work. His work is included in the collections of the Metropolitan Museum, the Art Institute of Chicago and Washington, University, St. Louis.

BEAUDIN, André. French School. 1895. (Page: 233.)—Born February 3, 1895, at Mennecy (Seine-et-Oise). Student at the Arts Décoratifs from 1911 to 1915. Since 1919 has exhibited at the Salon d'Automne, then at the Indépendants, and chiefly at the Surindépendants where, for many years, he, his wife Suzanne Roger, and Borès have formed a gathering center for the younger generations. An excellent engraver, he has illustrated several works.

BECKMANN, Max. German School. 1884. (Page: 317.)—Born in Leipzig, he was an artist from childhood on. Between 1900 and 1903, he studied with the Norwegian Frithjof Smith, later independently in European museums. Painted and taught in Frankfurt-am-Main until he fled to Amsterdam Nazi persecution. In 1947, he came to the U. S., now teaches at Washington University, St. Louis. In 1949, he won First Prize at the Carnegie Institute annual.

BENTON, Thomas-Hart. American School. 1889. (Pages: 303, 305.)—Born in southern Missouri, the son of a criminal lawyer, he did cartoons as a boy, studied art at the Chicago Art Institute and finally ended up in the Mecca of his day, the Left Bank in Paris. Here originated the revulsion against the School of Paris which formed his style. Benton returned to America, worked out a living as stevedore, book illustrator, ceramist. Work during the First World War as a draftsman gave further objectivity to his view. His reputation was made on a number of mural projects of which those in the Missouri State Capitol are the most important. His easel paintings have been widely reproduced, command large prices.

BERMAN, Eugène. School of Paris. 1899. (Pages: 312, 316.)—Born in St. Petersburg, Russia, he studied painting in Germany, Switzerland and France, at the Académie Ranson. Trips to Italy, starting in 1922, plus study of Palladian architecture helped form his style. In the mid-1920's he was co-founder of the Neo-Romantic school. In 1935, he came to America where he enjoyed rapid success. He has designed widely for the theater and is internationally represented in museums.

BELLOWS, George, Wesley. American School. 1882-1925. (Pages: 285, 290.)—An artist from childhood, Bellows was born in Ohio, went to its State University where his achievements in football did not divert him from his pursuit of art. From cartoonist on a local paper, he progressed to New York and study under Henri. His canvases and lithographs revealed a new, brawny, vital America that had nothing to do with European derivation. A member of the National Academy at the age of 27, he rounded out his reputation with landscapes, portraits, scenes of prize fights, remaining, until his early death characteristically American. Over twenty-five museums own his work.

BIERSTADT, Albert. American School. 1830-1902. (Pages: 147, 154.)—Born near Düsseldorf, Germany, Bierstadt came to Massachusetts as an infant. At 22, he returned to Düsseldorf to study painting and later worked in Rome. Upon his return to the United States, he became interested in the wild aspects of the West, painting the Rockies with German nineteenth century Romanticism.

BINGHAM, George Caleb. American School. 1811-1879. (Pages: 155, 164, 287.)— Born on a Virginia plantation, his family joined the westward migration, ending in Missouri. Apprenticed to a cabinet-maker, his first artistic efforts were on his own initiative. In 1837, he spent a few months at the Philadelphia Academy, then moved to Washington, where he painted politicians for a livelihood. On returning to Missouri, he embarked on the genre style for which he is celebrated. In 1856, he went to Europe for two years, polishing up his technique at Düsseldorf. His pictures of the frontier and Mississippi River life have great vitality and veracity.

BLAKE, William. English School. 1757-1827. (Pages: 16, 105, 106, 138, 255.)—A visionary from childhood, Blake began to study art at ten and at fourteen was apprenticed to an engraver until 1778. He then began to engrave illustrations for various magazines and also to paint, chiefly in watercolors. At the same time he wrote poetry of a mystical nature which he illustrated and engraved entirely on copper. Apart from his own works, he illustrated the *Book of Job* and these twenty-one engravings done when he was nearly seventy are considered his best work. He was engaged upon the illustration of Dante when he died.

BOCCIONI, Umberto. Italian School. 1882-1916. (Pages: 251, 253.)—Born in 1882 at Reggio (Calabria). In 1901 he settled in Rome where he met Severini and Balla who were still, along with Boccioni, under the influence of Divisionism. With them he founded pictorial Futurism, and spent some time in Paris in 1911 and again in 1912 for the first Futurist Exhibition. Shortly afterward he evolved toward a more and more accentuated dynamism and also undertook sculpture. He died in 1916 as a result of a fall from a horse during the war.

BÖCKLIN, Arnold. Swiss School. 1827-1901. (Pages: 133, 137).—The son of a dyer, Böcklin studied drawing at Basel where the works of Holbein awakened his vocation. Later he visited Brussels, Antwerp, Geneva and Paris. From 1850 to 1857, he lived in Rome and later worked at Hanover and Munich, returning to Rome for four years. He practised both painting and sculpture and was also interested in mechanics, even inventing a flying machine. From 1874 to 1885, he painted in Florence where he produced most of his Classical works, then until 1892 he lived in Zurich. Finally he returned to Italy where he died.

BONINGTON, Richard Parkes. English School. 1802-1828. (Pages: 97, 104.)—Brought up at Calais, Bonington began to study painting at an early age under Gros. At twenty he exhibited at the Salon with great success; two years later, at the famous Salon of 1824 where Constable won his fame, he was awarded a medal for his watercolors. In 1825, he visited England and Italy. Under the guidance of Delacroix, he turned to oil-painting and exhibited at the Royal Academy. At the height of his career he died of a sunstroke.

BONNARD, Pierre. French School. 1867-1947. (Pages: 92, 94, 95, 96, 167, 188, 257.)—His early vocation was opposed by his bourgeois parents and he was made to study law. At the same time, he continued painting and enrolled at the École des Beaux-Arts. At twenty-one he broke with his parents and struck out on his own, influenced chiefly by Gauguin, and exhibiting at the Salon des Indépendants. In 1900, he was already famous, and yet he changed his style completely, in order to put form in harmony with color. When the cross of the Legion of Honor was offered him, he refused, as Monet and Degas had done before him.

BORES, Francisco. Spanish School. 1898. (Page: 233.)—Born May 6, 1898, at Madrid. Took courses at the Madrid School of Fine Arts. Exhibited for the first time in 1922 at Madrid, and took part in the big exhibition of Modern Painting in 1925, also at Madrid. Arrived in Paris in 1925 and soon made the acquaintance of Picasso and Juan Gris. Since 1927 has exhibited at the Tuileries, then at the Surindépendants, and the Salon de Mai.

BOUDIN, Louis-Eugène. French School. 1824-1898. (Pages: 35, 42, 49, 63.)—The son of a ship's pilot, Boudin started life as a cabin-boy; at twenty he sold stationery at Le Havre. At twenty-five, he attracted the attention of the Havre town council and was sent to study art in Paris under Isabey. On his return he taught painting, and exercised a considerable influence on Claude Monet. While in Paris, he met Baudelaire and through him became friendly with Jongkind. In 1875, he joined the Impressionists. While earning his living as a farm laborer, he exhibited at Antwerp, Bordeaux and Dordrecht. Finally success came to him and he was able to travel in Italy and the Near East.

BRACKMAN, Robert. American School. 1898. (Page: 302.)—Born in Odessa, Russia, he came to America at the age of 12, studied under Bellows and later at the National Academy of Design, of which he became as associate in 1932. He has won many honors as a portrait painter.

BRANGWYN, Frank. English School. 1867. (Page: 109.)—Of Welsh ancestry, Brangwyn studied in London and developed his gifts by working with William Morris, the Pre-Raphaelite poet and painter. His first works were tapestry designs, genre paintings and scenes of London and Venetian life. Later he traveled in India and became a powerful colorist and etcher, interested especially in exotic scenery and industrial life.

BRAQUE, Georges. French School. 1882. (Pages: 188, 196, 202, 205, 209, 213, 214, 215, 249, 253, 272, 277, 284.)—Born at Argenteuil, May 1882. Son of a house-painter with artistic leanings. Brought up at Havre where as a young man he got to know Othon Friesz. Went to Paris in 1904, and attended the Académie Julian. He had much in common with Friesz, and their pictures had points of resemblance until 1908, in which year Braque met Picasso, and turned to Cubism. He worked in close association of ideas with Picasso, but parted company with him after the war. Braque has done décors and theatrical designs for the Russian Ballet.

BREITNER, George, Hendrik. Dutch School. 1857-1923. (Pages: 120, 123.)— Born at Rotterdam, he entered the Hague Academy in 1875. He underwent the influence of Jacob Maris and soon became the leading exponent of the Dutch Naturalist School. His coloring is powerful, though sombre. He went in chiefly for the portraying of crowded streets, horses and vehicles. His pictures of Amsterdam give an exact rendering of the peaceful and harmonious atmosphere which is that of the "Northern Venice"

BRIANCHON, Maurice. French School. 1899. (Pages: 228, 233.)—Born January 1899, at Fresnay-sur-Sarthe, entered the École des Arts Décoratifs in 1915, where he found much in common with Oudot and Legueult. Paints interiors and landscapes, and has done theater decorations.

BROWN, Ford Madox. English School. 1821-1893. (Pages: 104, 110.)— After studying painting at Antwerp, Brown went to Paris where he spent three years and painted some of his most dramatic works. He traveled in Italy and on his return developed a new style which influenced one of his pupils, Dante Gabriel Rossetti, and led to the foundation of the Pre-Raphaelite school. He illustrated books and designed stained glass windows, besides painting historical pictures and landscapes.

BURCHFIELD, Charles, E. American School. 1893. (Pages: 305, 307.)— Born in Ohio, he began at an early age to contribute by odd jobs to the family budget. After high school, he decided to become an illustrator, entering the Cleveland School of Art on a scholarship. After an unsuccessful attempt at living in New York, he returned to Salem, Ohio, designing wallpaper, painting the "American scene" in his spare time. His contribution to watercolor technique was considerable.

BURRA, Edward. English School. 1905. (Pages: 277, 281, 283.)—Born in London. 1921-1923 studied at the Chelsea School of Art and later at the Royal College of Art. Settled at Rye, Sussex. He has traveled extensively both in Europe, the United States and Mexico. He became a member of "Unit One." Has had several one-man exhibitions in London and has made designs for ballet.

C

CADMUS, Paul. American School. 1904. (Pages: 335, 336.)—Born in New York City, he studied at the National Academy and the Art Students League. After some experience in advertising and a trip abroad, he received in 1945, a Chicago Art Institute prize. A meticulous painter of frequently controversial subjects, he is an expert draftsman and etcher, has created ballet sets and a mural. Thirteen museums and public collections own his work.

CAILLEBOTTE, Gustave. French School. 1848-1894. (Pages: 50, 67.)— Caillebotte worked in Bonnat's studio and was admitted to the École des Beaux-Arts in 1873. Towards this time, he gave up official teachings and joined the Impressionists. In 1882, or thereabouts, under Monet's influence, he devoted himself to landscape-painting and carried out numerous views of the Seine at Argenteuil.

CARRENO, Mario. School of Paris. 1913. (Page: 322).—Born in Havana, he studied at home, in Mexico City and in Paris, where he came into the School of Paris orbit. Has had successful shows in the United States, France and Cuba. In the last few years, his style has changed, now deals with the Afro-Cuban themes of a strong native school. He is represented in important museums and collections.

CARRIÈRE, Eugène. French School. 1849-1906. (Page: 30.)—His early years were spent at Strasbourg, and he was nearly twenty when, he saw the lovely pastels of La Tour and became interested in painting. His exhibit at the Salon of 1876, was much talked of and he was commissioned to decorate the Hôtel de Ville and the Sorbonne. In 1900, at the Universal Exhibition he was awarded the Grand Prix.

CARROLL, John. American School. 1892. (Pages: 327, 329.)—Born in Wichita, Kansas, he determined on an art career while in his second year at the University of California. After study with Duveneck, he enlisted in the Navy in World War I, subsequently settling in Woodstock, N. Y. Carroll was awarded a Pennsylvania Academy Purchase Prize in 1924, won a Guggenheim traveling fellowship in 1926.

CASSATT, Mary. American School. 1845-1926. (Pages: 55, 162, 166.)— Born in Pittsburg of an originally French family, she was taken to France as a child, later returned to Philadelphia where she studied art at the Pennsylvania Academy. In 1868, she again went to France to study in art galleries and eventually settle in Paris, exhibiting at the Salons. Influenced by Degas, who was a close friend, she joined the Impressionist group, applying its technique to the mother and child subjects for which she is famous. She rarely returned to her native country but did much to further the understanding of Impressionism in America.

CATLIN, George. American School. 1796-1872. (Pages: 150, 155, 287.)— Born Wilkes-Barre, Pennsylvania, studied law, practicing drawing for his own amusement. Eventually he set himself up as a miniature painter, progressing to the rank of portraitist. Interest in the Indians took him on many frontier expeditions during the course of which he recorded their appearance and way of life. In 1837, he brought these paintings and many objects to New York and opened an Indian Gallery which caused a sensation and eventually was transported by the artist to England and the Continent. In Paris, in 1845, he received commissions from Louis-Philippe. A skilful showman, he published catalogues of his material and notes on his adventures, nevertheless suffered from fluctuating fortunes. Before his death, he made further expeditions to South America, the Aleutians and the West Indies documenting his travels as he went.

CÉZANNE, Paul. French School. 1839-1906. (Pages: 42, 48, 63, 67, 70, 71, 72, 73, 75, 77, 90, 92, 188, 237, 249, 291, 297.)—The son of a banker, Cézanne attended school at Aix together with Émile Zola. He showed an early interest in painting and, having passed his baccalaureate, was sent to Paris, but failed at the preparatory examination for entrance to the École des Beaux-Arts. He thereupon started copying the Old Masters at the Louvre and in 1874, exhibited with the Impressionists. Later he quarreled with them and never exhibited again. In 1879, he left Paris for good, having quarreled even with Zola who had always defended him. He traveled to Belgium and Holland, but never returned to Paris where his works were exhibited by Vollard. His work was not made known to the public at large until 1900.

CHAGALL, Marc. School of Paris. 1887. (Pages: 200, 203, 205, 239, 241.)— Born at Witebsk in Russia, 1887, of poor Jewish parents. Became a painter at the age of twenty; studied at St. Petersburg, and went to Paris in 1910. Joined the Cubist group which included Gleizes, André Lhote, Delaunay and Apollinaire. During the war, in Russia, he started an art-school at Witebsk (1917) and was compeled to leave it to go to Moscow in 1920, where he worked at stage-decoration for the academic Jewish theater of Leningrad. Returned to Paris in 1922. He is also an engraver and illustrator.

CHASE, William, Merritt. American School. 1849-1916. (Pages: 157, 165.)
—Born in Franklin, Indiana, he studied in Indianapolis and New York.
Assisted by friends, he was able to go abroad in 1872 for further study
at the Munich Academy, where Duveneck and Twachtman were his co-
pupils. In Spain, Chase copied Velazquez; in England he became a friend
of Whistler. Back in America, he taught at the Art Students League
and various other schools, exerting a marked influence on the succeeding
generation of painters.

CHASSERIAU, Théodore. French School. 1819-1856. (Pages: 16, 39, 40.)—
Brought to France at the age of two, Chassériau entered the atelier of
Ingres at ten. At seventeen he exhibited *The Return of the Prodigal Son*
and at nineteen, *The Chaste Suzanna*, both extremely mature works. In
1840, he went to Italy where Ingres was Director of the Villa Medici. On
his return, he was commissioned to decorate the Cour des Comptes and
several churches. He died at the early age of thirty-seven.

CHIRICO, Giorgio di. School of Paris. 1888. (Pages: 221, 223, 226, 250,
252.)—Born in 1888 at Volo (Greece) of Italian parents. Studied at
Athens, then at Munich. Lived in Paris from 1911 to 1915, returned to
Italy, traveled, and came back permanently to Paris in 1924. First
influenced by Italian art of the Quattrocento (architectural landscapes),
then by the Munich school (Böcklin and Hans von Marees), 1919-1923.
Became a Surrealist in 1930, but has now returned to representational
art. He is also a writer and art-critic.

CHURCH, Frederick E. American School. 1826-1900. (Pages: 146, 154.)—
Born at Hartford, Connecticut, he painted the Catskills as a member
of the Hudson River School. Later, he traveled to Labrador, South
America, Europe, painting exotic scenes which helped popularize the
romantic aspect of the native landscape school. His view of Niagara
Falls was celebrated.

COLE, Thomas. American School. 1801-1848. (Pages: 144, 148, 149.)—
Born in England, he came to Philadelphia at 19 to engage in a career of
wood engraving. Later he worked as an itinerant painter, in New York
receiving encouragement from Trumbull, Durand and Dunlap. Between
1829 and 1832, Cole worked in England and Italy. His Romantic vision
has had repercussions down to the present day.

COLQUHOUN, Robert. English School. 1914. (Pages: 277, 279, 280.)—
Studied at the Glasgow School of Art. With the aid of a traveling scholarship has worked in France and Italy.

CONSTABLE, John. English School. 1776-1837. (Pages: 11, 20, 32, 34,
67, 101, 102, 104, 105, 256, 259, 266.)—The son of a wealthy miller, he
studied at the Royal Academy, copying the Old Masters and the Dutch
landscape painters, but after exhibiting in 1802 he turned to the direct
representation of Nature. However his landscapes met with little success
and he was obliged to paint portraits for his living. In 1816, he married,
and in 1828 his wife inherited a large sum of money which enabled Constable
to cease portrait-painting and work exclusively on landscapes. Meanwhile,
in 1821, he had painted *The Haywain* (or "A Landscape—Noon") which
won him a triumph in Paris, and the admiration of Delacroix, and definitely
influenced French Romanticism and landscape painting.

COROT, Jean-Baptiste-Camille. French School. 1796-1875. (Pages: 19, 20, 29, 30, 32, 34, 35, 42, 55, 67, 166.)—Son of a milliner and an accountant, he entered the Rouen Lycée with a scholarship and was later employed as a draper's assistant in Paris. After studying under Michallon and Bertin he spent two years in Rome. In 1827, he returned to Paris and successfully exhibited his Italian paintings at the Salon. He returned twice to Italy, in 1835 and 1843; the rest of the time he worked at Barbizon, Ville-d'Avray and Mortefontaine, near Paris. His works gained universal recognition as early as 1851.

COURBET, Gustave. French School. 1819-1877. (Pages: 20, 28, 30, 33, 35, 36, 50, 99, 117, 128, 132.)—His parents were landowners and he studied law in Paris, but soon gave it up to learn painting. It took him several years to gain recognition at the Salon, where he finally exhibited in 1844. In 1849, seven of his canvases were accepted and he was awarded a gold medal. His career progressed smoothly until 1870 when he took part in the political agitation, which came to a head in the Commune insurrection. He was arrested for having destroyed the Vendôme Column and sentenced to imprisonment, while the Column was re-erected at his expense. Completely ruined he retired to Vevey.

COUTURE, Thomas. French School. 1815-1879. (Page: 8.)—Trained first by Gros and later by Delaroche, Couture obtained the Prix de Rome in 1837 and continued his studies in Italy. In 1844, he exhibited with great success and started a career as official painter and teacher. He wrote two treatises on painting, but the last years of his life were spent in retirement and he died almost forgotten.

CRAXTON, John. English School. 1920. (Page: 284.)—The son of Harold Craxton, the musician. Studied at Goldsmiths College and the Westminster School of Art. Has traveled and worked in Greece.

CROME, John. English School. 1768-1821. (Pages: 20, 100, 101.)—The son of a poor weaver, John Crome was almost entirely self-taught. He seldom left his native town, except to visit London where he exhibited at the Academy, and in 1814 to travel in Belgium and France. In 1803, he founded the Norwich Society of Artists which set a fashion; all his life he was devoted to landscape painting, the scenery being chosen from his immediate surroundings which he depicted with great directness in a personal and sensitive style.

CURRY, John, Steuart. American School. 1897. (Page: 305.)—Of Scotch descent, he was born in a Kansas hamlet, worked to contribute to the family income from boyhood on. Reproductions of old masters interested him in art. His art study at the Chicago Art Institute was supported by odd jobs, a successive year in Paris was financed by borrowed money. Patronized by Gertrude Vanderbilt Whitney, he eventually won a Second Prize at the Carnegie Institute, taught in Cooper Union and at the Art Students League, became Artist-In-Residence at the University of Wisconsin. He has executed important murals and has a good museum representation.

D

DALI, Salvador. School of Paris. 1904. (Pages: 221, 222, 314, 316, 327, 334.)—Born in Figueras, Spain, he showed precocity from childhood. Briefly he attended the Madrid School of Fine Arts. Following his first trip to Paris in 1928, he was associated with Miro and Picasso. A member of, but later disclaimed by, the Surrealist movement, he had sensational shows abroad before creating the Dream of Venus for the New York World's Fair amusement park. He settled in America in 1940 where he has had many shows, enjoyed much success, published several books, designed advertising, cooperated on moving pictures.

DAUBIGNY, Charles-François. French School. 1817-1878. (Pages: 20, 32, 35, 42, 49.)—His first teacher was his father, a mediocre landscape painter; later he studied under Delaroche and spent a year in Italy. He exhibited in 1838 and in 1848, but attained success only in 1857. His landscapes were painted from Nature and his studio was a boat on the Seine or the Oise near Auvers where he lived. During the Commune he traveled in England and Holland where he painted several fine pictures.

DAUMIER, Honoré-Victorin. French School. 1808-1879. (Pages: 20, 30, 37, 38, 310.)—His father was a poor glazier; when he was eight, the family moved to Paris and the boy ran errands until he was old enough to study the lithographer's trade. Meanwhile Lenoir taught him painting and he became a political cartoonist. He made remarkable lithographs and it was not until the age of sixty that he found time to paint. In 1877, he became nearly blind; Corot helped him and the State granted him a small pension.

DAVID, Jacques-Louis. French School. 1748-1825. (Pages: 7, 8, 9, 11, 13, 132, 141.)—His first master was his relative, François Boucher, who placed him in the atelier of Vien. In 1774, after several attempts, he obtained the Prix de Rome and the following year left for Italy. On his return to Paris he was at once elected to the Academy. He was one of the founders of the Institute. When Napoleon came to power, David was appointed his court painter, but on the restoration of Louis XVIII he was banished to Brussels where he remained until his death.

DAVIS, Stuart. American School. 1894. (Pages: 292, 293, 297.)—Born in Philadelphia, Davis was one of the moving spirits of the revolutionary Armory Show in 1913. Through his father, who was art director of the Philadelphia Press, he early associated with Sloan and Glackens. From 1910 to 1913, he studied with Henri. During World War I he engaged in map-making for Army Intelligence. He has created murals for a music hall, a radio station and a State University. An early exponent of abstract art, he is also a lithographer, designer, craftsman, writer and teacher. The Museum of Modern Art and the Whitney Museum of American Art are among a number that own his paintings.

DEGAS, Hilaire-Germain-Edgar. French School. 1834-1917. (Pages: 48, 60, 63, 66, 68, 69, 90, 166, 255.)—The son of a banker, he entered the École des Beaux-Arts in 1855 and exhibited in the Salon of 1865. During the war of 1870 he fought as a volunteer and later went to America, bringing back interesting canvases from New Orleans. In 1870, he abandoned the official Salon and in 1874 joined the Impressionists whom he had encouraged from the beginning of the movement. His favorite subjects were racing scenes and ballet dancers, but he was also a fine portrait painter. A man of versatile talents, he pursued art for pleasure rather than profit, and was an engraver and a sculptor of no mean repute.

DELACROIX, Ferdinand-Victor-Eugène. French School. 1798-1863. (Pages: 7, 11, 16, 22, 23, 24, 104, 105, 123, 125.)—The son of a distinguished diplomat, Delacroix acquired a liberal education. He failed in his first attempts to obtain the Prix de Rome, but in 1822 his *Dante and Virgil* revealed his extraordinary talent. *The Massacres of Scio*, which he repainted after having seen Constable's *Haywain*, placed him at the head of the Romantic school. He never went to Italy, but in 1832, he traveled to Morocco; on his return he decorated many famous buildings (the Apollo Gallery of the Louvre and the Library of the Chamber of Deputies may be mentioned). In 1857, he was elected member of the Institute. He was also a gifted writer and art critic.

DELAROCHE, Hippolyte, known as Paul. French School. 1797-1856. (Pages: 8, 123, 133.)—A pupil of Gros, he first exhibited in 1822 and two years later attracted attention by his *Joan of Arc before Cardinal Beaufort* while the *Death of Queen Elizabeth* won him fame in 1827. In 1832, after the *Princess in the Tower*, he was elected to the Institute and appointed professor at the École des Beaux-Arts. During a voyage in Italy he married the only daughter of Horace Vernet. His studio was famous and he had many gifted pupils to whom he imparted his qualities of fine draftsmanship and precision.

DELAUNAY, Robert. French School. 1885-1941. (Pages: 205, 212, 215, 218, 251.)—Born Paris 1885. At first an adherent of Pointillism, he took to Cubism about 1910. He devoted himself to research in simultaneous contrasts of color, christened *Orphism* by Guillaume Apollinaire. Later he studied the expression of speed and movement.

DEMUTH, Charles. American School. 1883-1935. (Pages: 297, 298.)— Born Lancaster, Pennsylvania, his delicate health precluded his entering the family tobacco business and he devoted himself to painting. Studied at the Drexel Institute and the Pennsylvania Academy, in 1904 went to Paris for two years. His first products were book illustrations, later he worked in watercolor and oil, producing many still-lifes and distinguished architectural compositions that show the influence of Cubism.

DENIS, Maurice. French School. 1870-1943. (Pages: 92, 94.)—Brought up in Paris, he entered the Académie Julian at the age of eighteen and fell in with Émile Bernard and the *Nabis*. Through the former he became influenced by Gauguin. From the beginning of his career he was a critic as well as a painter, and executed mural decorations as well as woodcuts. In 1894, he went to Italy and later often returned to Florence, Siena and Rome, where he painted on the same sites as Corot.

DERAIN, André. French School. 1880. (Pages: 168, 181, 182, 185, 186.) —Born at Chatou. When fifteen, he began to paint and entered Carrière's studio. In 1899, he joined forces with his fellow-countryman Vlaminck, and they worked together. In 1905, he worked with Matisse at Collioure and exhibited at the so-called *Salon des Fauves*. He showed landscapes of the Collioure neighborhood. Since 1905, he experiments with constructive stylization, despite digressions in the archaic manner (1912). Only after the war did he really study the nude. He has done numerous theatrical decorations: one of the best-known is the set for the Russian Ballet, *La Boutique fantasque*.

DESNOYER, François. French School. 1894. (Pages: 234, 236.)—Born September 30, 1894, at Montauban. Took courses at the Arts Décoratifs and worked at the Gobelins with Bourdelle. Exhibited at the Indépendants after 1922, then at the Salon d'Automne, at the Tuileries, and the Salon de Mai. In 1923, obtained the Blumenthal Prize, and, in 1949, the Prize for Contemporary Painting. Professor at the École des Arts Décoratifs since 1938. Has traveled in Spain and Czechoslovakia, and frequently sojourned in the South of France. Collaborated on the International Expositions of 1925 and 1937. For the latter he executed a large stained glass window and a decorative panel. In 1942, was in charge of the decoration of the town hall of Cachan.

DIAZ DE LA PENA, Narcisse-Virgile. French School. 1807-1876. (Pages: 20, 49.)—His parents were exiles from Spain who left him orphaned at ten. He lost a leg through a snake-bite and was obliged to take up a sedentary occupation; his artistic gifts made him turn to porcelain decoration. A painter in his spare time, he exhibited with success at the Salon of 1831. In 1844, he was awarded a medal, to be followed by many others. Influenced by Delacroix, he was the painter of Fontainebleau forest and inspired both Corot and Millet, as well as the other painters of the Barbizon School.

DIEGO, Julio de. School of Paris. 1900. (Pages: 330, 332.)—Born in Madrid, where he received his formal art training. In 1924, after a Paris period, he first came to the United States, later worked in Mexico on successive trips. In 1935, the Chicago Art Institute awarded him First Prize. He has worked in many mediums, including stage design, illustration and metal (for jewelry). Leading American museums own his work.

DOUGHTY, Thomas. American School. 1793-1856. (Pages: 142, 144, 147.)—Born Philadelphia, he exchanged a business career for study of art. Self-taught, he became a member of the Hudson River School, working exclusively at landscape painting.

DREWES, Werner. German and American School. 1889. (Pages: 330, 332.)—Born in Germany, the son of a pastor, he fought in the First World War, afterwards gravitated to the Bauhaus, first in Stuttgart, later in Dessau. In 1922, he took a trip to Italy and copied old masters in Spain. After much travel, to South America and around the world, he came definitively to America in 1930, taught at Columbia University, exerted influence on U. S. Abstractionists. He has shown internationally and is owned by many museums.

DUFY, Raoul. French School. 1877. (Page: 183.)—Born at Havre. Attended the École des Beaux-Arts there, then joined his compatriot Friesz. In Paris, he attended the École des Beaux-Arts (atelier Bonnet). At first influenced by Impressionism his work from 1901 (when he first exhibited at the Salon des Artistes Français) until 1908 was close to that of Matisse. He also studied Cézanne. His full originality became evident after the war. By trade a decorator, Dufy remained a decorative artist by choice. He has done designs for textiles, ceramics and tapestry. He spends his time between Paris, the Norman coast, Nice and Cannes. His watercolors are famous, and he has done designs for the cover of *Vogue*.

DUNLAP, William. American School. 1766-1839. (Page: 147.) — Born Perth Amboy, New Jersey. In 1784, he went to London to study under Benjamin West. On his return he became a portrait painter, a miniature painter and a part-time theatrical manager. Between 1814 and 1836, Dunlap traveled around New York as assistant pay-master to the militia, painting landscapes. He is the author of a unique book of art criticism dealing with his contemporaries and as a naturalist had considerable learning.

DUNOYER DE SEGONZAC, André. French School. 1864. (Pages: 186, 195.)—Born near Paris, he belongs to the Quercy family. Entered the École des Beaux-Arts 1901. Later pupil of Jean-Paul Laurens at the Académie Julian, then took lessons at the Académie de la Palette. Joined there Albert Moreau and Boussingault. After 1910, his style took shape in *Les Buveurs*. During the war he was a lieutenant in charge of the camouflage section with André Marc, Boussingault, Camoin, Puy and Dufresne as collaborators. From 1920 to 1926, worked in the Ile-de-France. Chiefly a landscape painter. Since 1926 he often visits the South of France (Saint-Tropez). Segonzac is also an etcher.

DUPRÉ, Jules. French School. 1811-1889. (Pages: 19, 20, 49.)—Like Renoir, he began as a porcelain decorator, in his father's workshop, and was practically self-taught. His first exhibit at the Salon attracted public attention. Later, in London, he studied the English landscape painters who greatly influenced his luminous style.

DURAND, Asher B. American School. 1796-1886. (Pages: 145, 149.)— Born in New Jersey, he began a successful career as an engraver, turning to portraits only in 1835. For several years, he practised in Washington. In 1840, he took a trip abroad. Following this, he confined himself to landscape, playing an important part in the Hudson River movement.

E

EAKINS, Thomas. American School. 1844-1916. (Pages: 155, 156, 162, 163, 165, 287.)—Born in Philadelphia, in whose Pennsylvania Academy of Fine Arts he received his first training, Eakins was a scientific realist to whom the study of medical anatomy was as much a part of art as a course on æsthetics. In 1866, he went abroad to study with Gérôme for two years, then visited Spain where he studied Velazquez. His career in Philadelphia was beset with difficulties and criticism. His portraits and scenes of life around him are of an almost startling sincerity. The teacher of Henri, Sloan and Glackens, he is the moving force behind the subsequent "Ashcan School".

EILSHEMIUS, Louis. American School. 1864-1941. (Pages: 326, 327.)— Born New Jersey, of Dutch descent, he was educated in Germany and Switzerland, at 17 returned to America, attempted a business career, studied agriculture, eventually turned to art, first at the Art Students League, then at the National Academy and at Julian's in Paris under Bouguereau. Working in America but unrecognized for nearly 30 years, he was "discovered" by Marcel Duchamp in 1917, since 1926 had many one-man shows, although by this time he had become a disappointed recluse.

ENSOR, James. Belgian School. 1860-1942. (Pages: 115, 246.)—His father was English and his mother of Flemish-Spanish stock. He began to draw at the age of fifteen and studied at the Brussels Academy from 1877 to 1881, the year of his first success. In 1884, he exhibited with the group of the XX. In 1888, he painted *The Entry of Christ into Jerusalem*, a huge canvas, over 40 ft. long and 14 ft. high, which brought him celebrity. From 1885 to 1904, he executed a great many engravings. In 1900, he was awarded a bronze medal at the Paris Exhibition. He is also known as a violently satirical writer.

ERNST, Max. German School. 1891. (Pages: 218, 221, 226, 239.)—Born at Cologne (Germany). Studied at the City University. Joined the Expressionist group "Der Sturm"; founded the Dadaist movement in Cologne in 1919. Became a Surrealist. Has lived in Paris since 1922. Is also an illustrator.

ESTÈVE, Maurice. French School. 1904. (Pages: 229, 233, 234.)—Born at Culan (Cher). After spending a year in Spain, he worked until 1927 at the Colarossi Academy. After 1928, has exhibited at the Indépendants, then the Surindépendants, at the Salon d'Automne, and the Salon de Mai.

ETTY, William. English School. 1787-1849. (Pages: 99, 100.)—The son of a miller and spice-maker, Etty worked as a printer's apprentice in Hull for seven years, studying art in his spare time. In 1807, he became a student at the Royal Academy, London, and was a pupil of Sir Thomas Lawrence for a year. His first success came in 1811 when two of his works were exhibited. In 1816, he made a short visit to Italy and in 1822 he went back for a year and a half during which time he studied the works of the great masters, being particularly attracted by the color of the Venetians. He was elected a member of the Royal Academy in 1828.

F

FANTIN-LATOUR, Ignace-Henri-Jean-Théodore. French School. 1836-1904. (Pages: 41, 42, 48.)—The son of a painter, he was trained by his father. In 1854, he entered the École des Beaux-Arts and at the same time worked in Courbet's atelier. His first exhibit at the Salon of 1861 was greatly admired; he had been rejected two years previously. He continued to send his paintings to the official Salon but also exhibited at the Salon des Refusés. He traveled in Belgium and England, as well as in Germany. His wife was also a painter.

FEININGER, Lyonel. German and American School. 1871. (Pages: 316, 317.)—Born in New York of German parentage, Feininger returned to Europe to study in Berlin, Paris, Brussels. From 1895-1900 he did cartoons, in 1913 he was associated with the *Blaue Reiter* movement. Between 1919 and 1924, he was an instructor at the Bauhaus. Now established in America, he has shown internationally and received many prizes.

FILLA, Emil. French School. 1892. (Page: 253.)—Born April 3, 1892, at Chropyne (Czechoslovakia). Worked in Prague before traveling around Europe. From France he retained a highly colorful and ardently lyrical

Cubism. Alfter having lived in Holland during the war, he took up residence in Prague where he has remained ever since.

FORAIN, Jean-Louis. French School. 1852-1931. (Page: 87.)—A pupil of Gérôme at the École des Beaux-Arts, he worked as a newspaper illustrator, and exhibited at the Salons of 1884 and 1885. He was influenced by Manet, Degas and the other Impressionists.

FREUD, Lucien. English School. 1922. (Page: 284.)—Studied sculpture at the London County Council School of Arts and Crafts, and painting and drawing at the East Anglia School of Painting and Drawing. Has traveled and worked in Greece.

FRIEDRICH, Caspar-David. German School. 1774-1840. (Pages: 127, 128.)—Born at Greifswald. Died at Dresden. This artist is typical of the German School in that he seeks above all, in his works, to express the romantic pantheism dear to his native culture.

FRIESZ, Othon. French School. 1879-1949. (Pages: 185, 186, 187.)— Born at Havre, Feb. 1879, of a sea-faring family. After taking lessons with a local artist named Lhuillier, he won a municipal scholarship and went to Paris to attend the École des Beaux-Arts, atelier Bonnat, where he met Dufy whom he had known as a boy. He became associated with Matisse, Derain, Picasso and especially with Braque. He perfected his technique after the First World War.

FUSSLI, Henry. Swiss School. 1741-1825. (Page: 138.)—A contemporary of William Blake, this Swiss painter, who worked mainly in England, first went to Italy in 1770 or thereabouts. On his return to London, he exhibited his canvas, *The Nightmare*, at the Royal Academy of which he became an associate in 1788. Milton's poems and Shakespearian drama were his main source of inspiration.

G

GALLATIN, Albert-Eugène. American School. 1881. (Page: 325.)—Born in Villa Nova, Pennsylvania, Gallatin belonged to a family of financial and political eminence. An early champion of the School of Paris, he did much to introduce their works into America and in addition patronized young American artists of forward tendency, founding the Museum of Living Art in 1927 for their benefit. Gallatin has had many exhibitions in Paris as well as in New York. He is the author of numerous books on artists and monographs, is an enthusiastic bibliophile.

GAUGUIN, Paul. French School. 1848-1903. (Pages: 80, 83, 84, 85, 86, 90, 91, 92, 94, 168, 185, 189, 239, 241, 249.)—His life was exceptional; after a childhood spent in Peru and an adolescence at sea, he became an assistant broker and settled down seemingly to a quiet married life. Entirely self-taught, he began painting in 1875 and suddenly realizing the strength of his vocation gave up his family for his art. After a sojourn in Denmark where he left his Danish wife and children, he lived for a time in Brittany, at Pont-Aven, then he traveled to Martinique. On his return, he met Van Gogh and quarreled with him; after a short period in Brittany he went back to the savage lands, this time to Tahiti. There he turned native and painted some of his most striking works. Illness brought him back to Paris, but he could no longer bear European life and returned to Tahiti for good in 1895. His works exercised a very great influence on 20th century art. Besides his paintings he also executed lithographs, woodcuts and sculpture.

GÉRARD, François-Pascal-Simon, Baron. French School. 1770-1837. (Pages: 7, 14.)—Brought to France at ten, he became the pupil of David at sixteen. His first exhibit in 1795 brought him to the fore at once. He devoted himself to portrait-painting and executed likenesses of the greatest celebrities. Napoléon commissioned him to paint historical pictures and so did Louis XVIII who appointed him First-Painter and raised him to the rank of Baron.

GÉRICAULT, Jean-Louis-André-Théodore. French School. 1791-1824. (Pages: 7, 11, 15, 17, 125.)—The son of a lawyer, he studied art first under Carle Vernet and then at the atelier of Guérin where he met Delacroix. He began to exhibit in 1814 and then went to Italy. In 1819, he created a sensation with the *Raft of the Medusa*, exhibited the following year in London. His drawings and lithographs show singular power. A fall from a horse injured his spine and he died eleven months later at the age of thirty-three.

GÉROME, Jean-Léon. French School. 1824-1904. (Page: 8.)—A pupil of Delaroche, he went to Italy with his master in 1844 and began to exhibit in 1847, with great success. In 1855, 1857 and 1846 he visited Turkey, Egypt, Algeria and Central Europe. In 1865, he was appointed Professor at the École des Beaux-Arts. Later he gave up painting and devoted himself to sculpture.

GLACKENS, William. American School. 1870-1938. (Pages: 285, 287.)—Of Philadelphia ancestry, Glackens was educated in his native town and studied art at the Pennsylvania Academy of Fine Arts. In 1895, he took leave of his newspaper illustrator's job to spend a year in Paris, where he came in contact with the Impressionists, Manet and Renoir. In 1898, he covered the Cuban hostilities for *McClure's* magazine. Soon after, he turned from black and white to color, becoming a member of the realistic group called "The Eight". His pictures present a unique record of the New York of the early 1900's.

GLEYRE, Charles. French School. 1806-1874. (Pages: 8, 42, 132, 136, 166.)—This artist, of Swiss origin, studied at Lyons and later in Paris, where his life was that of many poor students. After a sojourn in Italy, he exhibited his *Lost Illusions* in 1843. This was to be his last exhibition. Thenceforth he took over Delaroche's studio and taught painting with unselfish devotion.

GOERG, Édouard. School of Paris. 1893. (Pages: 194, 203.)—Born June 1893 at Sydney, N. S. W., of French parents who settled in Australia. He began painting shortly after he arrived in France in 1910. He attended the Académie Ranson where he was a follower of Maurice Denis (1912-1914). Later he was influenced by Daumier and Rouault.

GRANT, Duncan. English School. 1895. (Pages: 266, 267, 268.)—Born at Rothiemurchus, Inverness-shire. In 1902 began to study at the Westminster School of Art. In 1906 worked in Paris with Jacques-Emile

Blanche. He was an early member of the London Group, with whom he has exhibited consistently. In 1913, joined the Omega workshops organized by Roger Fry, the art critic, for the production and sale of applied art. Has been much in France, but lives close to the South Downs, Sussex.

GRAVES, Morris. American School. (Page: 330.)—Born in Fox Valley, Oregon, he moved to West Washington the following year. In 1930, he made a trip to Japan which aroused his first interest in Oriental art forms. In 1940, he went to Puerto Rico. In 1942, the Museum of Modern Art included a group of his works in a show which made him an overnight sensation. During the war, Graves remained a pacifist. He is the winner of a Guggenheim Fellowship which he spent in Europe. His work is owned by discriminating collectors.

GREENE, Stephen. American School. 1918. (Pages: 335, 336, 337.)—Born in New York, he studied at the National Academy of Design and the Art Students League. He obtained two scholastic degrees at the College of William and Mary and Iowa State University. He has taught at Indiana University and received a number of prizes, including the Prix de Rome in 1949.

GRIS, Juan. School of Paris. 1887-1927. (Pages: 205, 210, 211, 215, 239.)—Real name José Gonzales. Born Madrid. Died Boulogne-sur-Seine, 1927. His family had intended him to be an engineer, but he gave up his career, went to Paris in 1906, and settled at the "maison du bateau-lavoir", residence of many artists who afterwards became famous. He formed a close friendship with Picasso. His first paintings date from 1910.

GROMAIRE, Marcel. French School. 1892. (Pages: 193, 203.)—Born in 1892 at Noyelles-sur-Sambre (Nord). While studying law in Paris he took lessons in art at the Atelier de la Palette, where he was a pupil of Le Fauconnier. He was called to the colors in 1914, wounded in 1916, and had formed his style as an artist by about 1920. About 1923 he was doing scenes of peasant life. Exhibited *La Guerre* at the Indépendants, 1925. Has done landscapes, nudes, illustration work and etchings. He is a teacher at the Académie Montparnasse and one of the great masters of Expressionism.

GROPPER, William. American School. 1897. (Pages: 309, 310.)—Born in New York, his first study of art was in night hours between work in a sweatshop. Later he studied under Bellows and Henri. His second career as a cartoonist dates from 1919 when he worked as a newspaper artist on New York dailies. A well-known lithographer, he has illustrated over a dozen books, executed Government murals. In 1937, he received a Guggenheim Fellowship.

GROS, Antoine-Jean, Baron. French School. 1771-1835. (Pages: 7, 10, 11, 12, 24.)—A pupil of David, he showed remarkable talent but failed to obtain the Prix de Rome. In 1793 he traveled in Italy where he met Josephine Bonaparte who commissioned him to paint the general's portrait. Bonaparte took him into his favor and on his return to Paris continued to patronize him. Charles X also held him in great esteem and raised him to the rank of Baron. Gros, as a loyal disciple of David, was greatly perplexed by the progress of Romanticism, and attempted to return to Classic painting, but failed in his attempt and committed suicide by throwing himself into the Seine near his birthplace.

GROSZ, George. German and American School. 1893. (Pages: 237, 241.)— Born in Dresden. Studied there and in Berlin. Then served in the German army during the First World War. He returned to Berlin to create from 1918 to 1925 one of the greatest archives of satirical art of all times. Over thirty books of his works have been issued. He arrived in U.S.A. 1932 on the invitation of the Art Students League to teach there. Grosz has turned to watercolors and oils of American life; was granted a Guggenheim Fellowship; and had a one-man show in 1941 at the Museum of Modern Art.

GRUBER, Francis. French School. 1912-1948. (Paes: 233.)—Born in Paris; died in 1948. Son and brother of master-glassmakers. Studied from 1930 to 1939 at the Scandinavian Academy with Friesz, Dufresne, and Bissière. Became friendly with Tailleux, Despierre, Marchand, and Tal-Coat and exhibited with their group. Participated after 1930 at the Tuileries, Automne, and Salon de Mai of which he was a founding member. In 1938 executed the decoration of the Lycée Lakanal, in 1937 a stained glass window for the pavilion of the City of Paris, and in 1946 a tapestry cartoon.

GRUNEWALD, Isaac. Swedish School. 1889. (Page: 249.)—Born in Stockholm (Sweden). After beginning his career, he came to work under Matisse. Then settled in Paris until 1932 when he became a professor at the School of Fine Arts in Stockholm.

GUÉRIN, Pierre-Narcisse, Baron. French School. 1774-1833. (Page: 7.)—After his Prix de Rome, obtained in 1797, he remained in Paris, where he exhibited with great success in 1799. He then went to Italy, returning in 1802. From 1882 to 1829 he was director of the Villa Medici in Rome, where he remained until his death although ill-health prevented him from working. A pupil of Regnault, from whom he acquired his Classic style, he was the master of the leading Romantic painters. Géricault, Delacroix and Ary Scheffer.

GUSTON, Philip. American School. 1912. (Page: 330.)—Born in Canada, he came to California, studied at the Otis Art Institute in Los Angeles, made his apprenticeship on WPA murals and later taught art at the University of Iowa (1941-'45) and Washington University, St. Louis (1945-'47). In this last year, he won a Guggenheim Fellowship and in '48 received a grant entitling him to a fellowship in the American Academy in Rome. He has received half a dozen museum prizes.

GWATHMEY, Robert. American School. 1903. (Page: 310.)—Born in Richmond, Virginia, he studied at the North Carolina State College of Agriculture and Engineering, at the Maryland Institute and later at the Pennsylvania Academy of Fine Arts, which, in 1929 and '30 awarded him a Cresson Traveling Scholarship. Many prizes followed, including a Carnegie Institute award in 1942, a Rosenwald Fellowship in '44, a Pepsi-Cola prize in '46 and a grant from the American Academy of Arts and Letters. He has taught at Beaver College, Pennsylvania; Carnegie Institute; and at Cooper Union in New York City. Many leading museums have shown, and own, his work.

HARNETT, William M. American School. 1848-1892. (Page: 162.)—Born in County Cork, Ireland, he was brought to Philadelphia as a baby. A professional engraver, he studied at the Pennsylvania Academy in off hours and later in New York. In 1878, he went abroad to paint, exhibit and live four years in Munich. In the 1880's, he returned to America equipped with a realistic technique which permitted the *trompe l'œil* effects for which he was celebrated in his day and rediscovered in our time.

HARTLEY, Marsden. American School. 1877-1943. (Pages: 297, 299.)— Born in Lewiston, Maine, he moved to Cleveland for his art study and eventually won a scholarship at the Cleveland School of Art. In 1899 he came to New York, studied at the National Academy of Design. This was followed by considerable travel. In 1930, he won a Guggenheim Fellowship. His work is in America's leading museums.

HASSAM, Childe. American School. 1859-1935. (Pages: 159, 166.)—Of English-Puritan descent, the artist was born in Massachusetts, entered art via the engraver's workshop, became an illustrator. Three years' study in Paris brought him under the influence of the Impressionists, whose credo he thereafter expounded. In addition to landscapes, his street scenes are noteworthy.

HENNER, Jean-Jacques. French School. 1829-1905. (Page: 30.)—He studied art first at Altkirch and Strassburg, then in 1847 at Paris. In 1857 he returned to his dying mother and painted her on her death-bed as the Belgian painter Ensor was to do later. The following year on his return to Paris he obtained the Prix de Rome. A medal was awarded him in 1863 and he rose regularly in the ranks of the Legion of Honor until he became Grand Officier in 1903; while in 1889 he had been elected to the Institute.

HENRI, Robert. American School. 1865-1929. (Pages: 285, 288.)—Born in Ohio, his art study took him to the Pennsylvania Academy of Fine Arts, the Académie Julian and the École des Beaux-Arts, Paris. For another decade he worked independently in France, Italy, Spain, in Paris opening an art school jointly with William Glackens. Identified upon his return to America in 1900 with "The Eight" School of early Realists, Henri exerted great influence as a teacher for over thirty years.

HODGKINS, Frances. English School. 1869-1947. (Pages: 260, 261, 262.)— Born at Dunedin, New Zealand. Studied with her father, but chiefly self-taught. After her father's death, came to England in 1900. Visited France and Morocco. Taught watercolor painting at Colarossi's studio, Paris. 1912 returned to New Zealand and held exhibitions there and in Australia. She was again living in Paris when the 1914 war drove her back to England. 1919 began painting in oils. 1922 moved to Manchester, which she made her head-quarters for several years.

HODLER, Ferdinand. Swiss School. 1853-1918. (Pages: 134, 138.)—This artist, who acquired a reputation throughout Europe for his lofty and rugged figures, is the author of famous frescoes; during his younger days he likewise painted delicately suggestive landscapes.

HOLMAN HUNT, William. English School. 1827-1910. (Page: 105.)—One of the founders of the Pre-Raphaelite Brotherhood, Holman Hunt became a student at the Royal Academy in 1845. Three years later, after several successful exhibitions of genre paintings and illustrations of scenes from Dickens and Scott, he began working in the Pre-Raphaelite manner. In 1854, Holman Hunt went to Palestine to study Eastern life and following this visit and several others painted a number of pictures inspired by Biblical scenes.

HOMER, Winslow. American School. 1836-1910. (Pages: 150, 153, 154, 162, 287.)—Of Yankee stock, he was born in Boston. A lithographer apprentice, he soon began to contribute drawings to magazines. Briefly, he studied at the National Academy of Design on New York. During the Civil War, he was artist-correspondent for *Harper's Magazine.* His first paintings were genre subjects. Two European trips produced little effect on his style and, in 1884, he settled at Prout's Neck, Maine, to paint the sea pictures on which his reputation mainly rests. He also took trips to the Caribbean, the Adirondacks and Bermuda, producing important watercolors which represent a great technical advance over previous work in this medium.

HOPPER, Edward. American School. 1882. (Pages: 307, 310.)—Born Nyack, New York, of Dutch-English ancestry, he studied at the Chase School under Henri and Kenneth Hayes Miller for five years. In 1906 he went to Paris, earning his way as a magazine illustrator. The Armory Show gave him his start, later the Whitney Studio Club. Abandoning watercolor for oils in the 1920's, he achieved great success.

I

INGRES, Jean-Auguste-Dominique. French School. 1780-1867. (Pages: 6, 7, 8, 16, 25, 26, 27.)—The son of a talented painter, sculptor and musician, he entered the studio of David, in 1797. In 1801, he obtained the Grand Prix de Rome, but lack of funds delayed his journey to Italy until 1806. In 1824, he was commissioned to paint a picture for the Cathedral of Montauban and the resulting masterpiece, *The Vow of Louis XIII*, brought him fame, together with material independence. The following year he was elected to the Institute and was appointed professor in 1826. He remained in Paris until 1834 when he returned to Rome as the Director of the Villa Medici, the post having been vacated by Horace Vernet. Seven years later he returned to Paris and in 1856 exhibited *La Source*, one of his finest works, which he had begun thirty-two years previously. He attained the highest dignity, that of Grand Officier de la Légion d'Honneur in 1855 and was appointed Senator for life in 1862.

INMAN, Henry. American School. 1801-1846. (Pages: 151, 154.)—Born in Utica of English parents, he moved to New York at the age of 12 and soon started a seven-year apprenticeship to John Wesley Jarvis. Later President of the National Academy of Design, he resigned and eventually settled in Philadelphia. Primarily a miniature and portrait painter, he also painted romantic landscapes, though his later work tends towards genre. He died after a trip to England in 1884.

INNESS, George. American School. 1825-1894. (Page: 166.)—Born in Newburgh, he had a hard struggle with a shop-keeping father to follow an artistic career. Eventually, he received a few lessons and was apprenticed to an engraver. After study with Regis Gignoux, he went abroad, studied the old masters in Italy and contacted the Barbizon School. Back in America, he painted in a new spirit which eventually supplanted the Hudson River School. Although handicapped by ill health and financial discouragement, his work breathes poetry and delicacy. Inness died on a trip to Scotland.

ISRAELS, Josef. Dutch School. 1824-1911. (Pages: 119, 123.)—A pupil of Ary Scheffer, he was at first attracted by historical subjects, but soon found his real vocation in genre painting, depicting the life of the poor. His first success was obtained at the Paris Universal Exhibition of 1855; two years later, having left Paris and settled at Katwijk near Leyden, he sent to the Salon his *Children of the Sea* and in 1867 *The Interior of the Orphan Home at Katwijk* for which he was awarded a medal and the Legion of Honor. Later he took up residence at The Hague.

J

JOHN, Augustus. English School. 1879. (Pages: 264, 266.)—Born at Tenby, South Wales. Exhibited with the New English Art Club as early as 1899. Teacher of Art at University of Liverpool, 1901. In 1903 went to live in Essex. Did many drawings and paintings of gipsies in England, Wales, Ireland France and Spain. 1909 settled in Chelsa. 1921 elected member of the Royal Academy. He has visited America and spent much time in France. Principally a portrait painter, though also interested in figure composition and landscape.

JOHN, Gwen. English School. 1876-1939. (Pages: 265, 267.)—Born at Haverfordwest, Pembrokeshire; sister to Augustus John, the painter. Studied at the Slade School of Art. Moved to Paris and became a pupil at Whistler's School. Developed a close friendship with the sculptor Rodin. Passed the rest of her life in Paris or at Meudon. Died 1939.

JOHNSON, Eastman. American School. 1824-1906. (Page: 155.)—Born in Maine, he apprenticed to a Boston lithogapher. By 21, he was earning a living at doing crayon portraits. By 1849 he had earned enough money to go abroad, studying for two years in Düsseldorf, traveling in France and Italy, living for four years at The Hague, where he became interested in seventeenth-century Dutch genre. Invited to become Holland's court painter, he declined to return to America in 1855. In New York he completed the rural genre scenes for which he is best known and which were wideley distributed through engravings.

JONES, David. English School. — 1895. (Pages: 273, 275.)—Born at Brockley, Kent, 1909 became a student at Camberwell School of Art. Served in the 1914-'18 war and later published a book on his experiences, which was awarded the Hawthornden prize in 1938. In 1919 returned to his studies at Westminter School of Art. 1922 joined Eric Gill, the sculptor, in Sussex to work for the Guild of St Joseph and St. Dominic, described as a «company of craftsmen». Moved to Wales 1925. Returned to live at Brockley, Kent, 1927.

JONGKIND, Johann-Barthold. French School. 1819-1891. (Pages: 35, 42, 49.)—A pupil of Isabey, he exhibited in the Paris Salon of 1848, and in 1852 was awarded a medal. The world of art then forgot him and disappointed he ceased to exhibit in 1872, retiring to the Alps where he continued to paint until his death. Only then were his fine marines, landscapes and etchings appreciated. He excercised a great influence on Claude Monet and the other Impressionists.

K

KANE, John. American School. 1860-1934. (Page: 330.)—Born in Scotland, he worked as a child in the coal mines, arrived in America as an immigrant and went to work in Pittsburg as a mill-hand, street paver and house painter. A Sunday painter, he depicted the oddly industrialized country around Pittsburg in his off-hours, also fanciful and charming reminiscences of his homeland. After two rejections, one of his pictures was finally hung in the Carnegie International in 1927. Today he is prized as a leading American primitive.

KANDINSKY, Vasili. École de Paris. 1866-1944. (Pages: 239, 249, 250, 253.)—Born December 5, 1866, in Moscow. After scientific studies and a career at the University, he left in 1896 to study painting in Munich, and later traveled through Europe. In 1911, he turned toward non-objective art, in 1912 published *Uber das Geistige in der Kunst*, and participated in the *Blaue Reiter*. After remaining in Moscow from 1914 to 1921, he returned to Germany to become a professor at the Bauhaus in Weimar and then in Dessau. In 1933, he took refuge in Paris where he died in 1944. To-day he is recognized as one of the masters of abstract art.

KENSETT, John F. American School. 1818-1872. (Pages: 146, 150.)—Born in Connecticut, began artistic career as apprentice to an engraver uncle. By 1840, this profession permitted him to take a trip to Europe, visiting England, Germany and Italy. After seven years, he returned to paint studio-made landscapes over a successful quarter-century.

KLEE, Paul. Swiss School. 1879-1940. (Pages: 221, 226, 249, 254.)—Swiss painter, graphic artist and writer, born of Bavarian and French parents, near Bern, Switzerland, in 1879. Studied in Munich 1898-1900. Original member of the *Blaue Reiter* group, Munich, 1912. Professor, at the Bauhaus, 1920-1929. Under the influence of the art of children and primitive men, he painted highly sophisticated pictures. Claimed by both Dadaists and Surrealists, but always kept aloof from any movement. Resigned his professorship at the Düsseldorf Academy after the National Socialist revolution in 1933. Lived in Switzerland from then on until his death in 1940.

KNATHS, Karl. American School. 1891. (Pages: 291, 292.)—Born at Eau Claire, Wisconsin, he studied at the Art Institute of Chicago, later worked in New York and the artist's colony of Provincetown, which inspired some of his best-known subjects. In 1946, he won First Prize at the Carnegie Institute annual and two years later a purchase prize at the University of Illinois annual. The Phillips Memorial Gallery in Washington has an unusually comprehensive collection of his work.

KOERNER, Henry. American School. 1915. (Page: 335.)—Born in Vienna, he came to America in his twenties to become a citizen, producing posters for the Office of War Information during the war. Accredited to the Graphics Division of the Military Government in Germany, he held his first one-man show in Berlin in 1947, attracting much attention. He has received prizes from the National Foundation for Infantile Paralysis (poster) and the Temple Medal from the Pennsylvania Academy annual. Critics have acclaimed his work as outstanding.

KOKOSCHKA, Oskar. Austrian School. (Pages: 238, 241.)—Born in 1886, at Pœchlarn (Lower Austria). Studied in Vienna where he exhibited at an early date, at the same time as in Berlin where he was warmly received. Wounded during the war he settled in Dresden until 1924. Then he traveled continually throughout Europe, according to his troubled moods, producing moving evocations of the great capitals.

KROGH, Per. Norwegian School. 1889. (Page: 249.)—Born at Asgardstrand (Norway). Family of painters. As early as 1896 he went to study in Paris and was later to work with Matisse. His life was to be divided between Oslo and France, and he was likewise to execute numerous mural decorations in the respective capitals.

KUHN, Walt. American School. 1880-1949. (Pages: 293, 294, 297, 298.)—Born in New York, he studied art extensively in European countries, including Holland, Spain and Germany. He began his career as a cartoonist on a San Francisco newspaper, between 1908-1909 was instructor at the New York School of Art. In 1913, he was co-organizer of the Armory Show. A large traveling exhibit of his work has toured the country; he is represented in many museums. Kuhn also designed the interiors of railroad cars.

KUNIYOSHI, Yasuo. American School. 1893. (Pages: 295, 297, 327.)—Born in Okayama, Japan, he came to America in 1906, worked as fruit picker and itinerant laborer, studied in Los Angeles and later at the New York Art Students League, where he has since taught. From 1925 to '28 he traveled in Europe. Since 1934, he has received a succession of prizes, including a Guggenheim Fellowship and two Carnegie awards. The museums which own his work number nearly two score.

KUPKA, François. Czechoslovakian School. 1871. (Pages: 219, 239, 251.)—Born in 1871 in Bohemia. After studying in Prague, he went to Paris in 1894 where he settled permanently. After 1911, he oriented his work toward seeking rhythm alone, and, abandoning objective painting, he furthered his research by associating forms and colors.

L

LA FRESNAYE, Roger de. French School. 1885-1925. (Pages: 214, 219.)—Born at Le Mans July 1885; died at Grasse Dec. 1925. Descendant of an old Norman family, he entered the Académie Julian in 1903 and became associated with Segonzac, Luc-Albert Moreau, and especially Boussingault. He afterwards frequented the Académie Ranson, where he was taught by Maurice Denis and Sérusier. His own style began to form about 1909.

He died of pneumonia contracted during the war. His loss was one of the most serious which contemporary French art has sustained.

LAWRENCE, Jacob. American School. 1917. (Page: 311.)—Born in New Jersey, he studied at the American Artists School, won three Rosenwald Fellowships and a Guggenheim. In 1941, the Downtown Gallery exhibited a pictorial story of his race entitled *Migration* describing the difficulties of the Negro. This was reproduced by *Fortune* magazine and later jointly bought by the Museum of Modern Art and the Phillips Memorial Gallery. He has exhibited and is collected throughout the country.

LAWRENCE, Sir Thomas. English School. 1769-1830. (Pages: 98, 100.)— An innkeeper's son, he began to draw portraits at the age of ten. In 1787, entered the Royal Academy as a student and soon became famous as a portrait-painter. Elected an Academician in 1794. was knighted in 1815 and made President of the Royal Academy on the death of Benjamin West.

LAWSON, Ernest. American School. 1873-1939. (Pages: 163, 166.)—Born San Francisco while parents were traveling, the son of a doctor and of New England ancestry, Lawson in 1888 got his first art apprenticeship in Kansas City. The following year he went to Mexico as a draftsman on a canal project, there studied at the San Carlos art academy, saving money for two years in New York, working under Twachtman at the Art Students League, and a further year in Paris. In 1894, he returned to Connecticut, then lived in Greenwich village. In 1916, he traveled in Spain. He held many large exhibits including one in Paris, was awarded sixteen major prizes over his career.

LÉGER, Fernand. French School. 1881. (Pages: 175, 205, 209, 211, 215.)— Born at Argentan in 1881. Was an architectural draftsman and retoucher of photographs. Spent two years at the École des Beaux-Arts (1901-1903). Became interested in Cubism in 1908. His taste for mechanics and scientific research has induced him to bestow on a large number of his works a special flavor of "machinism". His film *Ballet mécanique* was an anticipation of the modern films of animated objects.

LEGUEULT, Raymond. French School. 1898. (Pages: 227, 233.)—Born May 10, 1898, at Paris. Entered the École des Arts Décoratifs in 1914 and, after the war, remained at the Ecole, along with Brianchon, until 1925. After 1921, exhibited at the Nationale, then at the Salon d'Automne, and at the Tuileries. Professor at the École des Arts Décoratifs from 1925 to 1944. Executed several decorative works; settings for the Opera (Grisélidis, Naissance de la Lyre, etc.); decoration of the Girls' School at Fontainebleau; tapestry cartoons...

LEIBL, Wilhelm. German School. 1844-1935. (Pages: 128, 130.)—Born at Munich, is main exponent of Realism in Germany. Chiefly remarkable for his graduated coloring and for the equanimity of his figures, he had a preference for rustic figures. He also painted numerous portraits.

LIEBERMANN, Max. German School. 1847-1900. (Pages: 132, 133.)— This artist is the main exponent of Impressionism in Germany. He abandoned dark and heavy hues for clear, light and aerial coloring. He was most at home in landscapes and portraits.

LHOTE, André. French School. 1885. (Pages: 216, 219.)—Born at Bordeaux, apprenticed to a sculptor-decorator in wood. Trained at the local school of Fine Arts. Came to Paris in 1907 and thanks to the generosity of an art-lover, the deputy attorney-general Granié, spent two years at the Villa Medici free. Became associated in 1911 with the Cubist Group, but never accepted the doctrine in its strictest form, and attempted to reconcile abstraction with nature. He still pursues this method. He is a theorist and teacher, head of an art-school in the Rue d'Odessa, at Montparnasse. Lhote has a considerable influence in contemporary students of art; he is a subtle and lucid writer and lecturer.

LUKS, George B. American School. 1867-1933. (Pages: 286, 287.)—Born in Pennsylvania of an artistic family, he trained at the Pennsylvania Academy. Later he studied in Düsseldorf, Paris, London, returning to become a newspaper illustrator, covering the Cuban revolt in 1895 and 1896. A member of *The Eight*, his painting represents earthy subjects taken from his own youth when wrestling and prize-fighting were dominant interests. His portraits, despite their rough subjects, are perceptive.

LURÇAT, Jean. French School. 1892. (Pages: 226, 235.)—Born at Bruyères (Vosges). First studied medicine, then began painting with the decorator Pourvé at Nancy. Came to Paris in 1910 and became associated with Vildrac and Élie Faure. After the war, traveled all over Europe and then in America. Is also an illustrator and a decorator, but chiefly designs tapestries. First living artist in this field in France, he is associated with the Aubusson factory.

M

MACBRYDE, Ian. English School. 1913. (Pages: 277, 280.)—Studied at the Glasgow School of Art. Won a traveling scholarship which enabled him later to work in Italy and France.

MACIVER, Loren. American School. 1909. (Page: 330.)—Born in New York City, she studied briefly at the Art Students League. *Fortune* and *Town and Country* magazines have published her illustrations. Her original "success of prestige" among connoisseurs has attained general proportions with over ten museums now owning her work.

MACKE, August. German School. 1887-1914. (Pages: 240, 249, 251.)—Born January 3, 1887, at Meschede in the Ruhr. After finishing his art studies, he made several trips to Paris and throughout Europe between 1905 and 1913. With Kandinsky and Marc he collaborated on the editing of the *Blaue Reiter*. A close friend of Delaunay, he too arrived at a highly colored Cubism. He was killed at the front in 1914, in Champagne.

MALEVITCH, Casimir. Russian School. 1878-1935. (Page: 253.)—Born in 1878 at Kiev. He successively underwent the rising influence of the Fauves and Cubists, and in 1913 founded *Suprematism*, in Moscow. After the war he traveled in Germany where he met Kandinsky at the Bauhaus. He died in 1935, at Leningrad.

MANET, Édouard. French School. 1832-1883. (Pages: 30, 41, 42, 43, 44, 45, 46, 47, 48, 50, 55, 60, 61, 134, 261, 263.)—The son of a magistrate, he went to Italy in 1853 and also visited Munich, Dresden and Prague, copying the Old Masters. He obtained his first success at the Salon of 1862, but really awakened public interest in 1864 at the Salon des Refusés. His fame grew steadily and his influence on the painters of his day was very great.

MANESSIER, Alfred. French School. 1911. (Pages: 231, 233, 234.)—Born December 5, 1911, at Saint-Ouen (Somme). Took courses in architecture at the École des Beaux-Arts for a while before going to work under Ranson where he met Bissière. Has exhibited since 1935 at the Salon des Indépendants, Salon d'Automne, Tuileries, and Salon de Mai of which he is a founding member. Executed several tapestry and stained glass window cartoons.

MARC, Franz. German School. 1880-1916. (Pages: 242, 249, 251.)—Born in 1880, at Munich where he pursued his studies in art. His first trips to Paris in 1903 and 1907 had a great influence on him. In 1911, he met Kandinsky, and together they published the manifesto of the *Blaue Reiter*. He was ardently interested in the study of animals, and, under the stimulus of Cubism as well as through his friendship with Delaunay, he finally arrived at a non-objective art in which color plays a major role. He was killed during the war in 1916, before Verdun.

MARCHAND, André. French School. 1907. (Pages: 232, 233, 234.)—Born February 10, 1907, at Aix-en-Provence. After secondary studies in his native town, he took evening courses in drawing from 1918 to 1923. Living in Paris since 1925, he works there alone. Travels and sojourns frequently in Provence, the South of France, Central Europe, and North Africa. In 1937 obtained the Paul Guillaume Prize. Exhibits, since 1931, at the Tuileries, Salon d'Automne, and Salon de Mai of which he is a founding member. Aided from the beginning of his career by Darius Milhaud for whom he executed the settings of the *Suite Provençale* and *Mireille*.

MARIN, John. American School. 1870. (Pages: 287, 291, 292, 297.)—Born in New Jersey, he studied at the Pennsylvania Academy of Fine Arts and the Art Students League, then worked in an architect's office. From 1905 to 1909, he traveled in Europe. A leading exhibitor at the Armory Show, he was soon identified with the advance-guard movement in the United States. The subject of many books and monographs, he is nationally represented in American museums. His innovating technique in watercolor has had a large following.

MARIS, Jakob. Dutch School. 1837-1899. (Pages: 116, 119.)—Extremely precocious, he was a student at the Hague Academy at the age of twelve. In 1866, Jakob exhibited at the Salon in Paris where he resided until 1870. After the war he settled at the Hague. Success came to him through the French firm of Goupil, one of whose directors was Théo Van Gogh, the brother of Vincent, who taught the public to appreciate the works of the Maris brothers.

MARIS, Thys. Dutch School. 1839-1917. (Pages: 117, 119.)—His art was totally different from his brother's, although their lives were parallel until 1870 when Thys enlisted in the National Guard and helped to defend Paris. In 1872, he went to London where he worked on stained glass. A third brother, Willem, developed a brighter but less original style (1844 1910).

MARQUET, Albert. French School. 1875-1947. (Pages: 179, 185, 186.)—Born at Bordeaux 1875. Arrived in Paris 1890. Became a student at the École des Arts Décoratifs, then at the Beaux-Arts in Gustave Moreau's studio, where he became associated with Matisse. After Moreau's death, he worked with Matisse in the Louvre. In 1902, he exhibited at Berthe Weil's, from 1904 onwards at Druet's. In 1906, he traveled by water in many parts of the world, in Europe, on the Mediterranean, in Morocco in 1912 with Matisse and Camoin, in 1920 in Algiers, in 1922 in Tunis, and in 1928 in Egypt. On his return to Paris, he painted the Paris quaysides he has always admired.

MARSH, Reginald. American School. 1898. (Pages: 304, 307.)—Born in Paris of American parents, Marsh inherited his talent from his painter father. Later, in New Jersey, he came in contact with many artists, including Bellows. At Yale he cartooned, later contributed to *Vanity Fair* and spent three years on the staff of *Harper's Magazine*. Influenced by Kenneth Hayes Miller, who was his teacher, Marsh turned to native subject matter. He has created murals and theater décor. In the last years, his preponderant interest has been drawing.

MATISSE, Henri. French School. 1869. (Pages: 172, 174, 183, 185, 186, 188, 205, 209, 213, 228, 233, 240, 249, 269, 277, 297.)—Born at Château-Cambrésis (Nord), Dec. 1869; went to Paris 1890. Entered the École des Beaux-Arts and became associated with Rouault, Marquet, Manguin and Camoin. In 1899, he met Derain, Puy and Laprade. He was well on the way to the realization of his aims by 1905 (Salon d'Automne) and became completely himself in 1906 (*La Joie de vivre*). His studio, the Couvent des Oiseaux, rue de Sèvres, was frequented by his students, notably the American Bruce and the German Hans M. Purrmann. In 1908, he moved his studio to the Couvent du Sacré-Cœur, expressed his doctrines in *A Painter's Notes*, a statement which became the charter of a new phase of European Art. In 1911, 1912, he traveled in Morocco and settled in Nice in 1917. Voyage to Oceania in 1931. In 1933, painted his most important decorative work for Dr. Barnes, Marion, U.S.A.

MASSON, André. French School. 1896. (Pages: 220, 221.)—Born at Balagny (Oise). Developed on his own, frequented Loutreuil. Exhibited for the first time in 1922, then with the Surrealist group from 1924 to 1928. Has executed several mural decorations, ballet settings, and a great number of illustrations.

MATTSON, Henry. American School. 1887. (Page: 327.)—Born in Gothenburg, Sweden, he came to the United States at 19, worked as a mechanic in Worchester, Massachusetts, taking night courses at the art museum. From 1916 on, he devoted himself to painting, settling in Woodstock, returning only once to the country of his birth. In 1935, he won a Guggenheim Fellowship. He has painted murals, is widely known for his marines.

MAUVE, Anton. Dutch School. 1838-1888. (Pages: 119, 121.)—Self-taught, he nevertheless remains with Jakob Maris and Israels one of the foremost Dutch artists of his time. He worked in oils and watercolors and exercised a definite influence upon his relative Vincent Van Gogh whom he taught for a short time.

MEISSONIER, Jean-Louis-Ernest. French School. 1815-1891. (Pages: 11, 192.)—Strongly attracted to art from childhood, he entered the atelier of Léon Cogniet and in 1834 exhibited at the Salon. His success encouraged his father to send him to Italy. After the Italian campaign in which he took part (1859), he became an historical painter. The greatest honors were awarded him during his lifetime; he was elected to the Institute in 1861 and in 1889 was President of the International Jury of Fine Arts.

MENZEL, Adolf-Friedrich-Erdmann. German School. 1815-1905. (Pages: 128, 138.)—He studied at the Berlin Academy and worked in every medium, being particularly known for his oil-paintings and drawings. He was also a lithographer and illustrator. In 1885 his 70th birthday was celebrated by an exhibition of all his works at the Berlin Academy.

MERIDA, Carlos. Mexican School. 1893. (Page: 322.)—Born in Guatemala of Spanish and Indian ancestry, at 17 he went to Europe for study and travel. Upon his return, he visited first the United States, then joined the group of mural artists in Mexico who were identified with the new movement in decoration. In 1930 his style became more abstracted and at the same time Surreal. He has exhibited in Mexico, Paris and all over America, and also done stage design.

MICHALOWSKI, Piotr. Polish School. 1804-1855. (Page: 125.)—This Polish painter of military scenes was born at Cracow in 1804. He is chiefly remembered as a watercolorist. Circumstances obliged him to seek refuge in France where he became a close friend of Horace Vernet and Charlet. He died in 1855.

MILLAIS, Sir John Everett. English School. 1829-1896. (Pages: 105, 107, 109.)—Amazingly precocious, Millais began the study of drawing at the age of nine and was admitted to attend the Royal Academy courses at eleven. Not long after, he founded the Pre-Raphaelite Movement with Holman Hunt and Dante Gabriel Rossetti, and adopted a new style of painting. However, in 1870 his manner changed again and, though technically perfect, became less interesting. He was created a Baronet in 1885 and elected President of the Royal Academy a few months before his death.

MILLET, Jean-François. French School. 1814-1874. (Pages: 20, 28, 31, 35, 41, 49, 58.)—Of peasant stock, Millet began the study of art at twenty and in 1837 entered the studio of Delaroche in Paris. He earned a precarious living by painting portraits and Bible scenes, and exhibited for the first time in 1840. In 1848, he went to live at Barbizon where he remained until his death. He traveled in Switzerland and also went to London. Only in 1867 was he recognized as one of the greatest painters of his time.

MINTON, John. English School. 1918. (Pages: 282, 284.)—Studied at the St. John's Wood Art School, London. Teacher at the Camberwell School of Art.

MIRO, Joan. School of Paris. 1893. (Pages: 221, 224, 225, 226, 239, 324.) —Born Barcelona 1893. Student at the Academy of Fine Arts, then the Academy Gali, both at Barcelona. Has been living in Paris since 1919.

MODIGLIANI, Amedeo. School of Paris. 1884-1920. (Pages: 186, 201, 203, 205, 239.) — Born at Leghorn in 1884. His father was a banker.

While still very young, he took to painting, studying at the Academy in Venice and in the Museums. He arrived in Paris in 1906, established himself in Montmartre, and soon experienced extreme poverty. He returned for a few months to Italy in 1909. He then took to sculpture. In 1913 he left Montmartre for Montparnasse. He died exhausted in 1920. His mistress, Jeanne Hébuterne, killed herself on hearing of his death.

MONDRIAN, Piet. School of Paris. 1872-1944. (Pages: 239, 246, 253, 316.) — Born March 7, 1872, at Amersfoort (Holland). After his art studies he began to work and in 1910 left for Paris where he underwent a strong Cubist influence. In Holland for the duration of the war, he, Theo Van Doesburg, and several other artists founded Neo-Plasticism in 1917, with the magazine *De Stijl*. He returned to Paris in 1918, remaining there until he left for London in 1939, and shortly thereafter for New York; he died in 1944.

MONET, Claude-Oscar. French School. 1840-1926. (Pages: 7, 20, 41, 52, 50, 52, 53, 54, 55, 60, 63, 67, 92, 105, 133, 166, 168.) — During his youth spent at Le Havre he taught himself painting and was encouraged by Boudin who gave him lessons. In 1862 he went to Paris and entered the studio of Gleyre but soon left it, with the other young painters he met there, and founded the Impressionist movement. In 1865 he exhibited for the first time at the Salon; in 1871 he went to London where he studied Turner and Constable. In 1874 he exhibited with the other Impressionists. From 1886 onwards he remained at Giverny and his works were greatly appreciated. He traveled in England, Holland, Norway and Italy. The last years of his life were spent in retirement, painting his famous lily-pools which may still be seen at Giverny.

MONTICELLI, Adolphe - Joseph - Thomas. French School. 1824-1826. (Page: 30.) — His family was of Italian origin; he studied painting at Marseilles and first went to Paris at the age of twenty-three. In 1856 he met Diaz whose influence may be seen in his works. The war of 1870 made him retire to Marseilles where he remained until his death.

MORAN, Thomas. American School. 1837-1926. (Pages: 149, 154.) — Born in Lancashire, England, he was brought to Philadelphia at the age of seven. His profession of wood engraver and illustrator alternated with attempts at oil paintings. He made various trips abroad, studying the masters and especially the works of Claude Lorrain and Turner. In 1871, he was commissioned by the Government to accompany and record an expedition to the Yellowstone region. His grandiose pictures of the West made his reputation.

MOREAU, Gustave. French School. 1826-1898. (Page: 196.) — The son of an architect, he entered the Ecole des Beaux-Arts in 1846 where for a time he was a pupil of Chassériau. He first exhibited in 1852, and his fame grew steadily until 1888, when he was elected to the Institute. Of independant means, he never sold any of his pictures, but left them to the State.

MORISOT, Berthe. French School. 1841-1895. (Pages: 44, 52, 60, 61, 67) — A grand-daughter of Fragonard, she studied unter Manet whose brother she married. She exhibited in 1864 and 1873, her works showing the influence of Corot. In 1874 she took part in the Impressionist Exhibition with Monet, Renoir and Sisley.

MORRIS, George L. K. American School. 1905. (Page: 325.)—Born in New York, attended Yale University and made his specialized training at the Yale School of Fine Arts and the Art Students League. Later he worked with Léger and Ozenfant in Paris. His literary interests brought him the editorship of *Partisan Review* and later of the Paris publication *Art Aujourd'hui*. He has shown publicly since 1935, participating in important group exhibitions, acquired by adventurous museums. His techniques include oil painting, fresco and sculpture.

MOUNT, William, S. American School. 1807-1868. (Pages: 148, 154.)— Born on a farm in Long Island of an artist and sign-painter family, he trained for three years at the National Academy of Design. He created early scriptural scenes and children's portraits, but is best known for a genre type of work drawn directly from his early rural surroundings. His work was reproduced by foreign lithographers and by Currier and Ives in America.

MUNCH, Edward. Norwegian School. 1863. (Pages: 246, 248.)—Born December 12, 1863, at Hedemark (Norway). Studied in Oslo, then made several extended visits to Paris, Italy, and Germany. Marked at the beginning by Impressionism and the School of Pont-Aven, he freed himself from their influence and obtained a great success in Germany. At Oslo, where he was to remain until his death, he executed several decorations and a great number of lithographs.

MUNKACSY, Michael Lieb known as MITSALY. School Hungarian. 1844-1900. (Pages: 123, 125.)—Left an orphan at an early age, he was apprenticed to a turner in Vienna where he learned to paint and later worked for a copyist of old pictures. In 1868 he studied in Düsseldorf and in 1872 took up residence in Paris. He exhibited in 1870, 1874 and the following years, and obtained a medal in 1878. After that date, he organized private exhibitions of his works, mainly genre pictures of Hungarian and Parisian life as well as some portraits and historical scenes. He traveled in Italy, Spain and Holland. Three years before his death he was stricken with insanity.

N

NASH Paul. English School. 1889-1946. (Pages: 272, 273.)—Born 1889. In 1907 decided to become an artist. Exhibited with the New English Art Club. Exhibited paintings of the battlefields at the Leicester Galleries, 1918. Took up theatrical design, wood engraving and book illustration. Taught at the Royal College of Art. Traveled widely. In 1933 took a leading part in the formation of a new group of English artists, who adopted the name "Unit One." Exhibited with the International Surrealist exhibition, London, 1936. Appointed an official war artist 1940. Died 1936.

NICHOLSON Ben. English School. 1894. (Pages: 272, 273.) Born at Denham, Bucks, the son of the painter Sir William Nicholson. Studied one term at the Slade School of Art. Visited Tours, Milan, Madeira and Pasadena, California, where he continued his studies. Returned to England 1918. Visited Paris and saw work of Cubists 1922. In 1926-1933 painting semi-abstract still-life groups. 1934 met Dutch painter Mondrian in Paris. Member of the Association Abstraction-Création 1933-1934.

NICHOLSON William. English School. 1872-1949. (Pages: 262, 263, 272.)—Born at Newark-on-Trent. Studied for a short time at the Herkomer School of Art, and later at Julian's in Paris. Produced a large series of woodcuts, the most famous of which is a portrait of Queen Victoria 1893. A successful portrait painter, he lived principally in London. Died, 1949.

NOLDE, Emil. German School. 1867. (Page: 241.)—Born August 7, 1867, in Schleswig. After his art studies in Germany and Switzerland, he traveled through Europe. At Dresden in 1905 he joined the "Die Brücke" group with whom he exhibited his violently colored canvases characterized by increasingly fantastic visions. His development in this vein was accentuated by his trip to Japan and the South Seas in 1913-1914.

O

O'KEEFFE, Georgia. American School. 1887. (Page: 297.)—Born in Sun Prairie, Wisconsin, she studied at the Art Institute of Chicago and the Art Students League in New York. In 1906, she abandoned art for nearly ten years, working in advertising agencies, teaching drawing in the public schools of Texas. A discovery of Alfred Stieglitz, who gave her first show at his gallery, she eventually married him. Her pictures bring high prices, are prized by museums.

OROZCO, José-Clemente. Mexican School. 1883. (Pages: 317, 320, 322.) —Born Jalisco, Mexico, studied first to be an agricultural engineer and later at the Fine Arts School. His first exhibition was held in 1915 in Mexico City. His early works consist of caricatures of political implication which made it necessary for him to leave for California in 1917. In 1919 he returned, soon began to paint murals, in 1922 he joined the Siquieros Syndicate. In 1930 he returned to California to create a decoration for Pomona College. This was followed by murals for the New School for Social Research in New York and an even larger wall decoration for Dartmouth. The political nature of his work has made it highly inflammatory.

OVERBECK, Johann-Friedrich. German School. 1789-1869. (Page: 126.) —The son of a magistrate, he received a good education and entered the Vienna Academy in 1806. With some friends he rebelled against the pseudo-classical teaching of the Academy and was expelled. In 1809 he went to Rome where he founded the German Pre-Raphaelite School, together with Cornelius, Schadow, Schnorr and Veit. He attracted the critics' attention in 1811 by a picture of the Madonna; in 1813 he became a Catholic. In 1819 an exhibition of paintings by German artists in Rome brought him fame. He executed a great many frescoes and engravings of religious subjects.

P

PASCIN, Julius. School of Paris. 1885-1930. (Pages: 199, 203, 205, 239.)— Born at Widdin (Bulgaria) in 1885. His father was a Spanish Jew named Pincas, and his mother was Italian, born in Serbia. Finished his studies in Munich about 1900, and went to Paris in 1905.   Took part in various publications.   Went to America in 1914, and became an American citizen. Has traveled a great deal in Florida and Cuba.   In 1918, he married Hermine David in New York, and settled in Paris in 1920, leaving afterwards on further travels.   Restless, depressed, and a prey to private anxieties he committed suicide in June, 1930.

PASMORE, Victor.   English School.   1908.   (Pages: 261, 262.)   The son of a doctor, he was educated at Harrow.   He studied painting in his spare time and worked at the Central School of Art.   Exhibited with the London Group 1931 and elected a member 1933.   Left the Civil Service 1938 to devote his whole time to painting.

PECHSTEIN, Max.   German School.   1881.   (Page: 241.)—Born at Zwickaw (Germany), he studied in Dresden and soon joined with the "Die Brücke" group.   During his stay in Paris in 1907 he was impressed by Matisse, Gauguin, and exotic art.   Having become the best-known of the Expressionists, he traveled in Italy, and in 1914 made an extended visit to the South Seas.   After the war he traveled a great deal in Switzerland, France, and Italy.

PEIRCE, Waldo.   1884.   (Pages: 302, 303.)—Born in Bangor, Maine, the son of a well-to-do father, he went to Harvard in 1906, later to Paris to study art at the Julian Academy, and to Spain for travel.   During World War I, he drove an ambulance, received the Croix de Guerre.   When he returned to America, it was to settle in Maine, contributing to national art exhibitions, owned by many museums including the Metropolitan.

PENE DU BOIS, Guy.   1884.   (Page: 302.)—Born in Brooklyn, he studied at the New York School of Art under Chase and, from 1905-'06 at Colarossi's in Paris.   A reporter and music connoisseur, he became art critic for the *New York Tribune* and the *New York Post*, and later editor of *Arts and Decoration*.   From 1924-'30 he lived and painted in France.   He won many prizes including both First and Second Altman Prize at the National Academy and the Harris Silver Medal at the Art Institute of Chicago. Author of books and articles, formerly he taught at the Art Students League, now has classes in Connecticut.

PERMEKE, Constant.   Belgian School.   1886.   (Pages: 244, 25.)—Born at Antwerp.   Worked in Bruges and then at the Academy of Ghent where he met Van den Berghe and through him De Smet with whom he was to paint after 1908.   After Laethem-Saint-Martin, he went to live in Ostend where he was to remain permanently except durng the war when he was wounded and evacuated to England   It was there that his Expressionist conceptions developed with all their brutal force.   Back again in Ostend, he was to devote himself thereafter to depicting with harshness and grandeur the life of both fishermen and peasants.

PEUSNER, Antoine.   Russian School.   1886.   (Page: 253).—Born at Orel (Russia), he studied at Kiev and St. Petersburg before going to Paris in 1911 and again in 1913.   Taking refuge in Norway, with his brother Gabo, during the war; both Peusners returned to Russia in 1917, and Antoine worked with Malevitch.   It was in Germany, where he fled in 1923, that he began to practise sculpture.   Soon afterward, he settled permanently in Paris.

PICASSO, Pablo. School of Paris. 1881. (Pages: 168, 204, 205, 206, 207, 208, 209, 211, 213, 214, 215, 239, 249, 253, 272, 277, 279, 284, 322.)—Born at Malaga in October 1881, his father Ruiz Blasco, from a Basque family, was a drawing-master, whereas his mother came from a Genoese family named Picasso. Pablo started painting at thirteen and entered the Ecole des Beaux-Arts of Barcelona in 1895. He arrived in Paris in 1900. Until 1904, he worked partly in Spain and partly in Paris. Established himself in Montmartre in 1904, in the famous "bateau-lavoir." Became associated with Max Jacob, Van Dongen, Guillaume Apollinaire, Derain, Braque and Matisse. First Cubist paintings 1906-1907. Settled in Montparnasse 1912. Did the setting and costumes for Cocteau's ballet "Parade," music by Eric Satie, in Rome, 1917. Spends his time between Paris and the South of France. Is Director of the Prado Museum.

PIGNON, Édouard. French School. 1905. (Pages: 230, 233, 234.)—Born at Bully (Pas-de-Claias). Spent his entire childhood at Marles-les-Mines. Enrolled in an evening drawing course, he was a pupil of Auclair, then of the sculptors Arnold and Wlérick. Has exhibited since 1932 at the Indépendants, Tuileries, Surindépendants, and the Salon de Mai of which he is a founding member. Executed a decorative panel for International Exposition of 1937, and a decoration for the Girl's School at Creil in 1941.

PIPER, John. English School. 1903. (Pages: 276, 277, 284.)—Born at Epsom, Surrey. Educated at Epsom College. On his father's death in 1928 he left the family firm to become a painter. Exhibited Zwemmer Gallery 1933. Visited Paris during the same year and met Braque, Léger and Brancusi. Gave up painting to work on "constructions." 1938 returned to painting. 1940 appointed an official war artist. 1943 designed sets and dresses for the ballet "The Quest," designed for Old Vic productions and for Benjamin Britten's opera "The Rape of Lucrece."

PIPPIN, Horace. American School. 1888-1946. (Page: 333.)—Born West Chester, Pennsylvania, he did manual work until invalided after World War I, when he began painting. Discovered by important patrons in an amateur how in 1938, this Negro artist soon received one-man exhibitions in Philadelphia and New York. Included in the Museum of Modern Art's "Masters of popular Painting" show in 1938, he is recognized to-day as America's leading primitive, with many museums owning his work.

PISSARRO, Camille. French School. 1831-1903. (Pages: 42, 52, 57, 58, 59, 60, 67, 76.)—His parents were Portuguese. He went to Paris during his childhood and studied art first under Melbye and then under Corot. In 1852 he traveled in Venezuela, while in 1870 he took refuge in London where he particularly studied Turner and Constable. Millet and Monet both exercised a great influence upon him. He exhibited from 1859 to 1870. Later he lived in the country near Gisors and exhibited at the Salon des Indépendants. He also executed pastels and etchings.

POLEO, Hector. Mexican School. 1918. (Pages: 319, 332.)—Born in Caracas, Venezuela, he showed his precocity as a child when he entered the School of Plastic Arts at 11. At 19, he went to Mexico to study mural techniques, studying in all three years. His first American one man show in 1945 was rewarded not long after by a Guggenheim fellowship. He has since exhibited in the Latin-American countries and the United States.

POLLOCK, Jackson. American School. 1912. (Pages 324, 327.) Born in Cody, Wyoming, Pollock was one of the discoveries of the Works Progress Administration. His artistic training prior to this was with Thomas Benton and at the Art Students League. The Museum of Modern Art is one of the galleries that own his pictures.

PORTINARI, Candido. Brazilian School. 1903. (Pages 322, 323.) Born Brodoswki, Brazil, of Italian parents who were coffee workers. At 14 he journeyed to Rio, went to art school, supporting himself by executing photographic portrait drawings and eventually portrait commissions. 1928 he received the Prix de Voyage, went to France, Italy, England, Spain. Back in Rio, he gained a fashionable following as a portraitist in 1932. 1935, received Honorable Mention at Carnegie International. In '36 he became a member of the Faculty of Rio's University. From '38 on he has executed extensive, important public mural commissions.

PRUD'HON, Pierre-Paul. French School. 1758-1823. (Page: 11.)—The tenth child of a poor stone-cutter, was sent to the Dijon Art School at sixteen. Encouraged by a generous patron, the Baron Joursanvault, he went to Paris; three years later he left for Rome, where he remained for another three years. Back in Paris, he was noticed by Bonaparte at the 1801 Salon and his career was thus given a definite impulse. A thoughtless word, to the effect that if his wife died he would never remarry, made her commit suicide two years before his own death.

PUVIS DE CHAVANNES, Pierre. French School. 1824-1898. (Pages: 16, 40.)—Born in a cultured family, he was studying for an engineer's diploma when he fell ill and was sent to Italy for a rest. In 1850 he exhibited at the Salon but the following years his pictures were rejected and he did not exhibit again until 1859. Two years later he was recognized by the public and the State as the greatest mural decorator of the century, with the exception of Delacroix, and commissioned by town councils in Paris, Lyons, Marseilles, Boston and elsewhere. In 1896, he married Princess Marie Cantacuzène, but his happiness was brief; she died in 1898 and he followed her shortly after.

Q

QUIDOR, John. American School. 1800-1881. (Page: 150.)—Born in New York State, he was a co-pupil with Inman of John Wesley Jarvis. Unsuccessful as a portrait painter, he decorated coaches and fire-engines, finally finding his genre in illustrations of the Hudson River tales of his friend Washington Irving, to which he brought a unique spirit of satire and fantasy.

R

RAIN, Charles. American School. 1911. (Page: 334.)—Born in Knoxville, Tennessee, he was educated in Lincoln, Nebraska. Following study at the Art Institute of Chicago, he went to Europe in 1933, to work in Berlin and study the masterpieces in museums. His originally abstract technique changed over this period to one of minute realism. Hailed as one of the first Magic Realists, his work has been widely shown from New York to San Francisco and is importantly collected.

REDON, Odilon. French School. 1840-1916. (Pages: 30, 77, 92.)—A pupil of Gérôme, Redon soon freed himself from his master's classical teaching and developed in his own manner. He began as an etcher and lithographer, publishing a series of albums; later he worked in oils and pastels, also.

RENOIR, Pierre-Auguste. French School. 1841-1919. (Pages: 41, 42, 52, 61, 63, 64, 65, 66, 67, 92, 133, 168, 261, 303.)—Brought to Paris in his early childhood, the son of a poor tailor, Renoir upon leaving school earned his living by decorating porcelain. In 1858, he entered the studio of Gleyre where he met Monet, Bazille and Sisley. In 1864, he first exhibited at the Salon. The Impressionist Exhibition in 1874 brought him "notoriety" equal to that of his friends. Later he exhibited privately and his success grew year by year. He visited Italy, Spain and North Africa, and finally settled in the South of France.

ROSSETTI, Dante, Gabriel. English School. 1828-1882. (Pages: 108, 109.) —His father was an Italian poet who settled in London where he taught Italian in King's College. All his brothers and sisters were highly talented and he himself began to study painting at the age of fifteen. At the Royal Academy he met Millais and Holman Hunt, and founded with them the Pre-Raphaelite Brotherhood. He exhibited in 1849 and in 1850. Besides painting both in oils and in watercolors he wrote poetry. For the ten years preceding his death he lived as a recluse in spite of universal admiration.

RICE-PEREIRA, Irene. American School. 1907. (Page: 326.)—Born in Boston, she studied at the Art Students League in New York and subsequently abroad. Sponsored originally by the Guggenheim Museum of Non-Objective Art, she is now generally recognized as one of the leading innovators of the abstract medium. In 1946, she was awarded prizes in the Pepsi-Cola and La Tausca shows.

RIVERA, Diego. Mexican School. 1886. (Pages: 307, 318, 322.)—Born in Guanajuato, Mexico, he began his studies at the age of ten and continued them in Spain. Visiting Paris in the early twentieth century, he came in contact with Picasso espoused Cubism, traveled extensively, came home to become a leader in his country's modern art revival. He has painted over 300 murals, including the leading decorations of his native land and several controversial commissions in the United States.

ROBERT, Leopold. Swiss School. 1794-1835. (Pages: 132, 135.)—After studying under David in Paris, he proceeded to Italy and was the first modern painter to choose Italian models (often from the Roman slums) without transforming them into saints and madonnas. A journey to Naples put the finishing touch to his palette. His pictures enjoyed great success.

ROUAULT, Georges. French School. 1871. (Pages: 176, 177, 185, 196.)— Born at Belleville, 1871; he left primary school at fourteen, became apprenticed to a stained-glass maker; and attended the evening classes at the École des Arts Décoratifs. He entered Gustave Moreau's studio, where he remained, for five years, as favorite pupil. About 1896, Rouault began to paint landscapes; he renounced the academic style. Then he became interested in depicting traveling theatrical companies and circuses, street-scenes and street-walkers. He took to pottery making, then to engraving in black and color for book illustration. He has written art-criticism, poetry and memoires.

ROUSSEAU, Henri, called "the DOUANIER" (i. e. customs official). French School. 1844-1910. (Pages: 189, 190, 192, 333.)—Born at Laval, in 1844. Died in Paris September 1910. He was a customs official, always attracted by painting. After his retirement in 1886, he devoted himself entirely to painting. He was also a musician and a writer. He founded an Academy, called the Polytechnic Association, where he taught painting, music and recitation. He exhibited regularly at the Salon des Indépendants from 1886 onwards. He became known and appreciated by artists like Derain, Vlaminck and Picasso at the end of his life, and also knew the writers A. Jarry, G. Apollinaire, Max Jacob, Jules Romains and Georges Duhamel.

ROUSSEAU, Théodore. French School. 1812-1867. (Pages: 20, 21, 49.)— From the first, his aim was to paint landscapes after the manner of Hobbema and Ruisdael. After a successful exhibit at the Salon of 1831, he was rejected in 1835 and thereupon retired to Barbizon, where he worked until his death. Success came to him in 1849; he was given a commission by the State and was appointed President of the artistic Jury at the Exhibition of 1867.

RUNGE, Philip Otto. German School. 1777-1810. (Page: 127.)—One of the best-known, German romantic painters. Author of tales based on German folklore. The bulk of his work consists in landscapes and portraits.

RYDER, Albert Pinkham. American School. 1847-1917. (Pages: 325, 327.) —Born in New Bedford, Massachusetts, an old whaling town, he retained his interest in the sea throughout his long and often tragic career in New York. Largely self-taught, Ryder lived the life of a recluse, unmindful of the art around him or of the wishes of clients. Two short European trips failed to change his distinctive style whose out-and-out Romanticism seemed like an aftermath of earlier work and at the same time a forecast of modern schools. He exhibited at the National Academy of Design and also at the Armory Show, but was only appreciated after his death.

S

SARGENT, John Singer. American School. 1856-1925. (Pages: 165, 166.)— Born in Florence of American parents, Sargent was from the first an international, studying art all over the Continent, in 1874 entering the studio of Carolus-Duran. At 21, a likeness of his master was admired at the Salon; in 1884, his $M^{me} X...$ provoked a controversy. His master-piece is a group of seven portraits of members of the Wertheimer family in London's National Gallery. Popular on two continents, he painted the fashionable world with brilliance and sophistication. A series of mural decorations in Boston occupied him for a quarter century.

SCHADOW, Wilhelm von. German School. 1789-1862. (Pages: 127, 128.) —Another member of the Nazarene School, he later became director of the Fine Arts Academy at Düsseldorf.

SCHNORR VON CAROLSFELD, Julius. German School. 1794-1872. (Pages: 128, 129.)—A member of the Nazarene School, he worked at Munich and Dresden chiefly on religious productions and frescoes. He likewise illustrated the Song of the Niebelungen.

SÉRUSIER, Paul. French School. 1865-1927. (Pages: 91, 92.)—Born 1865; died at Morlaix 1927. About 1889, when bursar at the Académie Julian, he gathered round him several young artists whose talent he guessed (Bonnard, Vuillard, Maurice Denis, Roussel, Rousseau and Piot) and gave them as a group the name *Nabis* (enthusiasts). He introduced the group to Gauguin and his theories. Sérusier remained always interested in the ethical aspects of æsthetic problems. His influence on the development of contemporary art of every sort is now believed to have been very important.

SEURAT, Georges-Pierre. French School. 1859-1891. (Pages: 35, 74, 76, 78, 79, 90, 249.)—An artist from childhood, Seurat studied at the École des Beaux-Arts. After a period of drawing in black and white, he was attracted by the atmosphere of Barbizon and painted on the banks of the Seine and by the seashore at Honfleur. His favorite haunt was the island of La Grande-Jatte on the Seine near Paris. He was long misunderstood and his *Circus* exhibited at the Salon des Indépendants in 1891 met with no success. An exhibition organized in 1905 of all his works together with those of Van Gogh brought recognition to both artists.

SHAHN, Ben. American School. 1898. (Page: 314.)—Born in Kaunas, Lithuania, he came to the United States at the age of eight. He majored in biology at New York University and City College, evincing his first interest in art as a social campaigning medium in connection with the Sacco-Vanzetti and Mooney trials. Once a lithographer, later an assistant of Diego Rivera, he has painted numerous murals and has held important one-man shows. A number of advance-guard museums own his work.

SHEELER, Charles. American School. 1883. (Pages: 296, 297.)—Born in Philadelphia, of Welch-Irish parents, Sheeler studied at the School of Industrial Art and later with Chase at the Pennsylvania Academy. Represented in the Armory Show, he pointed the way to the appreciation of the American Scene through his renditions of industry. As a photographer, his work is outstanding, paralleling and influencing his art career. In 1945, the Art Institute of Chicago awarded him the Harris Prize. Leading museums own his work.

SICKERT, Walter Richard. English School. 1860-1942. (Pages: 255, 259, 266.)—Born in Munich, Germany. His father a Danish painter, his mother English. In 1868, his family moved to England where he was educated. 1886, New English Art Club founded with Sickert a member. Opened school in Chelsea. 1900, opened a school in Paris. Returned to England 1905. These years till 1914 known as his Camden Town period. Exhibitions Paris 1907 and 1909. Camden Town Group formed 1911. 1913 group enlarged and renamed the London Group. 1924 elected member of the Royal Academy. Taught in Royal Academy Schools 1926. 1934 made a full academician but resigned next year. 1938 moved to Bath. Died 1942.

SIGNAC, Paul. French School. 1863-1935. (Pages: 76, 90.)—Born in Paris, 1863, and died there in 1935. His vocation for art declared itself at an early age, and as soon as he was eighteen he abandoned the career of an architect, for which his family had destined him, for that of a painter. He was first attracted by the Impressionists, especially so in view of their revolutionary prestige. After this he allied himself with Seurat. In 1884, he became one of the founders of the Salon des Indépendants and was elected president in 1908. Signac was almost as much of a sailor as a painter. In 1892, he discovered St. Tropez so celebrated among artists in after years. In 1899, he published his book *From Eugène Delacroix to Neo-Impressionism*, which defined the doctrine of the school. Signac has left us glorious visions of the sea in various aspects from the North Sea to the Black Sea, but most of all of the Atlantic and the Mediterranean. The preliminary watercolors he often makes for his oil-paintings are quite as fine as the finished pictures.

SIQUEIROS, David Alfaro. Mexican School. 1898. (Page: 322.)—Born Chihuahua, Mexico, studied at the San Carlos Academy and Martinez Open Air School. Founder of the Centro Arte Realiste Moderno Painter, muralist and graphic artist, he is noted for his technical innovations which include the use of Duco and encaustic.

SISLEY, Alfred. French School. 1839-1899. (Pages: 42, 52, 55, 56, 57, 67, 133, 261.)—Of English parentage, Sisley has always been considered a French painter, having spent all his life in France. His teachers were Corot and Courbet. He also worked in the atelier of Gleyre where he met Renoir and Monet with whom he founded the Impressionist School.

SLEVOGT, Max. German School. 1868-1932. (Pages: 132, 134.)—One of the most important German Impressionists with Corinth and Liebermann, he went in for landscape, still-life and portrait painting, together with vast historical and mythological scenes. His work is alive and vigorous.

SLOAN, John. 1871. (Pages: 285, 289.)—Born in Pennsylvania, he moved to Philadelphia as a boy, later worked in this city in a bookseller's shop studying art at the Pennsylvania Academy. For three years, he was on the staff of the Philadelphia Inquirer, later contributed to the *New York Herald* and the *Philadelphia Press*. In 1905, he moved to New York supported himself by illustration and posters. From 1914 to 1930, he taught at the Art Students League, eventually becoming its president.

SLUYTERS, Jan. Dutch School. 1881. (Pages: 241, 245, 247.)—Born at Bois-le-Duc. After art studies in Amsterdam, he made a profitable, extended visit to Paris in 1906 and was strongly impressed by the works of Gauguin and Toulouse-Lautrec. Living in Amsterdam from that time on, he abandoned himself to an often dramatic lyricism.

SMET, Gustave de. Belgian School. 1877. (Pages: 243, 245.)—Born at Ghent, he studied and lived there until 1904 when he settled in Laethem-Saint-Martin along with Permeke and numerous other artists. Taking refuge in Holland during the war, he underwent the influence of Le Fauconnier and the German Expressionists. On his return to Belgium after the war he took part in the foundation of the group "Sélection" which brought together the Belgian Expressionists. However, once settled in the country of the Lys he soon abandoned his violent manner and returned gradually to a vigorous naturalism.

SMITH, Matthew. English School. 1879. (Pages: 268, 269, 270.)—Born at Halifax, Yorkshire. His father was the head of a wire business. At 17 Mathew entered a Bradford wool mill, and at 18 the family business. After some years left the business and studied painting at the Slade School of Art. Two years later he went to France and joined the school of Henri Matisse in Paris. Worked in France until the outbreak of war, 1914. First exhibited in 1915 with the London Group. Served in the forces and was wounded. Returned to Paris after 1918 and spent much time in Provence.

SOLANA, Jose. Spanish School. 1886. (Page: 249.)—Born at Madrid where he received his training and where he has continued to work and exhibit. A friend of the writer Gomez de la Serna, he has also published several books which are devoted, like his paintings, to evoking the most typical scenes from the life of the people of Madrid.

SOUTINE, Chaïm. School of Paris. 1894. (Pages: 197, 198, 203, 205, 239, 292.)—Born at Smilovitchi, province of Minsk, Lithuania, in 1894. Son of a tailor. His childhood was spent in poor circumstances. At twelve years of age he ran away to Vilno, earning his living as a photographer's assistant, while he took lessons in drawing. In Paris, in 1913, he entered the Ecole des Beaux-Arts, atelier Cormon, and became associated with Modigliani. After Modigliani's death, he lived at Céret (1920-1923), then at Cagnes, and returned eventually to Paris. He lives apart in closely guarded solitude.

SOYER, Raphael. American School. 1899. (Page: 307.)—Born in Tombov, Russia, of an artistic family, he came to the United States at the age of ten. At first he sold newspapers, worked in factories, studying at night in Cooper Union, at the National Academy and at the Art Students League under Du Bois. He has won an Honorable Mention at the Carnegie exhibition three times, as well as prizes and awards at the Corcoran Gallery, the Art Institute of Chicago, the Pennsylvania Academy. Soyer created a mural for the Philadelphia post office and his canvases hang in various museums.

SPEICHER, Eugene. American School. 1883. (Pages: 301, 303.)—Born in Buffalo, Speicher showed precocious talent from early childhood. Despite his interest in athletics, he determined to be an artist and after high school entered the Albright Art Gallery night classes while working in a lumber yard by day and playing baseball regularly. With an Art Students League scholarship, Speicher came to New York City, studying under Chase and Henri. By 1920, he was well established as a portraitist. He lives mainly in the artists' colony at Woodstock, painting still-lifes, portraits and figure compositions, represented in over two dozen museums.

SPENCER, Stanley. English School. 1892. (Pages: 271, 273.)—Born at Cookham, Berkshire, where he has mostly lived. Studied at the Slade School of Art 1910-1914. In the 1914-1918 war served as a Red Cross orderly and as a soldier in Macedonia. Has painted many easel pictures, often depicting Biblical subjects, with the village of Cookham as background; but his most important works are the wall paintings in the memorial chapel of Burghclere, Berkshire, which commemorate the soldiers of the 1914 war and depict their life on campaign.

STEER, Philip Wilson. English School. 1860-1942. (Pages: 256, 257, 259.) —Born at Birkenhead; the son of a portrait painter. Worked at figure composition and portraits during the winter months and every summer was spent in the English countryside painting landscape. 1903, appointed a professor of painting at the Slade School of Art. He continued to teach there till 1930. By this time his sight was beginning to fail, and by 1935 both his eyes were badly affected. A memorial exhibition held in the National Gallery 1943.

STEVENS, Alfred. English School. 1817-1875. (Pages: 109, 112.)—The son of a painter, he was sent to Italy in 1833 and remained there nine years, studying sculpture. Later he taught architectural drawing, residing at Liverpool and in London, executed a great many mural decorations, besides sculpture and portraits.

STEVENS, Alfred. Belgian School. 1828-1906. (Pages: 48, 114.)—After having studied in Brussels and Paris, he became exclusively a painter of feminine figures and particularly the Parisienne. Success came to him at once; in 1890 he was elected member of the Société Nationale des Beaux-Arts and was awarded the Grand Prix at the Universal Exhibitions of 1889 and 1900. He also became Commander of the Legion of Honor and acquired the highest Belgian distinctions.

STUEMPFIG, Walter. American School. 1914. (Pages 327, 328.)—Born Germantown, Pa., he studied at the Pennsylvania Academy from 1931 to 1935. In 1933 he was awarded a Cresson Traveling Scholarship. Since his first one-man show in 1942, he has enjoyed much success and become nationally known and collected.

SUTHERLAND, Graham. English School. 1903. (Pages: 277, 278, 284.) —Studied at Epsom College, Surrey. Studied at the Goldsmith's School of Art 1919-1925. 1927 appointed to teach etching at the Chelsea School of Art; 1935 also teaching composition and book illustration at the same school. In 1936 began to concentrate on painting and developed his present style. Appointed an official war artist 1940.

T

TAMAYO, Rufino. Mexican School. 1899. (Pages: 321, 322.)—Born in Oaxaca, Mexico, of Zapotec Indian ancestry, he completed his education as an agricultural engineer before entering the School of Fine Arts in Mexico City. After teaching in the primary schools, he became head of the plastic arts section in the Ministry of Education and eventually fine arts professor in 1928. Tamayo's frescoes are in the National Conservatory and the National Museum. Since 1926, he has held increasingly successful one-man shows in New York City. Recently, he made his first trip to Europe. Tamayo's work figures in distinguished collections.

TCHELITCHEW, Pavel. School of Paris. 1898. (Pages: 316, 317.)—Born in Moscow, he made his first artistic apprenticeship in Berlin, later came to Paris to become one of the founding members of the Neo-Roman art movement. Tchelitchew has produced highly imaginative and revolutionary stage settings, drawings of great distinction, controversial paintings. In 1942 the Museum of Modern Art honored him with a one-man show. Now an American citizen, he is equally well known in European capitals

THON, William. American School. 1906. (Page: 327.) Born in New York, this artist was virtually self-taught, attained several prizes which culminated in 1947 in a Fellowship in the American Academy in Rome. In 1949, the National Academy of Design awarded him a watercolor prize. He is a regular exhibitor at national annuals, has held many New York one-man shows and can claim museum buyers.

TOULOUSE-LAUTREC, Henri de. French School. 1864-1901. (Pages: 88, 89, 90, 93.)—Toulouse-Lautrec was descended from the famous Counts of Toulouse. Two accidents during his youth arrested the growth of his legs and turned him into a grotesque dwarf. He left the country, and started to paint the life of the Parisan night-clubs and cafés. He found an endless variety of subjects in the Moulin-Rouge, and other cabarets. His work displays the keen perception and the exact drawing of the finest Japanese prints, and it also recalls the art of Degas: there is a kind of purity in his pitiless observation.

U

UTRILLO, Maurice. French School. 1883. (Pages: 186, 191, 192.)—Born December 1883. Son of Suzanne Valadon. He was an illegitimate child, and was recognized, as a matter of courtesy, by the Spanish writer Miguel Utrillo, in 1891. Began to paint about 1903, under his mother's direction. His difficult life was interrupted at intervals by periods in the hospital, made necessary by cerebral derangement. He now leads a calm life.

V

VANDERLYN, John.—American School. 1775-1852. (Pages: 140, 141.)— Born in New York State, he worked in a New York print-seller's shop at 17, studying art at night. Through the assistance of Aaron Burr, he studied under Stuart in Philadelphia and eventually went to France working for five years under Antoine Paul Vincent. In 1815 he returned for good, painted many prominent figures including four presidents He was disappointed, however, in his ambition to paint historical canvases.

VAN DONGEN. School of Paris. 1877. (Pages: 180, 185, 186, 247.)—Born at Delfshaven near Rotterdam. Son of a sailor. In 1897, after painting a few landscapes and fort-scenes in Holland, he went to Paris and took lodgings in Montmartre, living under conditions of great hardship. Gradually his circumstances improved. He left Montmartre for Montparnasse. He took an interest in every kind of subject: portraits, landscapes, interiors and still-lifes, and was perhaps fondest of all of flowers. After the last war, he became a fashionable artist.

VAN GOGH, Vincent. Dutch School. 1853-1890. (Pages: 80, 81, 82, 90, 91, 118, 123, 185, 239, 297.)—The son of a poor minister, he worked from the age of sixteen to twenty as a clerk in a firm of picture-dealers. His vocation thus awakened, he began to draw, but it was not until much later that he had the opportunity to study at Brussels and The Hague. In the meantime he tried to be a lay preacher, but without success, and lived like a tramp, unbalanced by several unhappy love affairs. His younger brother

Theo brought him to Paris where he met most of the Post-Impressionists. In 1887 he went to the South of France and lost his reason after a quarrel with Gauguin. After a period at a mental institution, he committed suicide.

VERESTCHAGIN, Vassili. Russian School. 1842-1904. (Pages: 124, 125.) —After finishing his studies at the Naval School in St. Petersburg, he turned to art and became a pupil of Gérôme in Paris. He took part in the Turcoman campaigns (1867) and the Russo-Turkish war (1877) which gave him material for striking paintings. He visited India twice and there also set down his impressions both with brush and pen, being a gifted writer. He was killed during the Russo-Japanese war.

VERTES, Marcel. School of Paris. 1895. (Pages: 315, 316.)—Born Budapest, he became a self-taught caricaturist and journalist of some renown. Fought First World War, afterward went to Paris where supported himself by book illustration. In 1935 he had a one-man show at the Petit Palais. In 1940 he came to America, achieved wide success as a magazine illustrator. Vertès has designed distinguished sets for ballet and theater, also fabrics, screens, ceramics. He has also executed two important private mural commissions, is known as a lithographer and painter.

VILLON, Jacques. French School. 1875. (Pages: 205, 215, 217, 219, 251.) —Born at Damville (Eure). Abandoned humoristic drawing in 1910, and somewhat under the influence of his young brother Marcel Duchamp, followed, the path of Cubism. In 1911 he founded with several friends the "Section d'Or "at whose meetings and dinners gathered La Fresnaye, Delaunay, Kupka . . . After the war, he earned his livelihood by his engravings. And from 1922 to 1933 he was engaged in solitary research. After 1935, and especially since 1940, his art has become freer, but is still subtly constructed upon color and light.

VLAMINCK, Maurice de. French School. 1876. (Pages: 168, 184, 185, 186, 292.)—Born at Paris 1876; his parents were teachers of piano and violin. His ancestors were Flemish and Dutch. A fine athlete, he was self-taught as a painter earning his living, by giving violin lessons: in 1899 he became associated with Derain, then with Matisse. An exhibition of the works by Van Gogh made a great impression on him. Exhibited for the first time in 1905 but did not devote himself entirely to painting until 1911. Not much of a traveler, he lived at Chatou, Bougival, and, since 1925, at Verneuil-sur-Avre. He is watercolorist, etcher and potter. As a decorator he has done cartoons for tapestry.

VUILLARD, Édouard. French School. 1868-1940. (Pages: 92, 94, 169, 171.)—A pupil of Bouguereau at the Académie Julian and later at the Beaux-Arts, Vuillard exhibited at the 1889 Salon where he obtained his first success. Later he joined the Salon des Indépendants. He was influenced by Maurice Denis and Paul Sérusier.

W

WALKER, Ethel. English School. 1877. (Pages: 258, 259, 266.)—Born in Edinburgh. No stereotyped art education in her youth; worked in museums. At 35 first went to an art school. Attended evening classes under Walter Sickert.

WATTS, George Frederick. English School. 1817-1904. (Pages: 109, 113.)—Practically self-taught, he won prizes for the decoration of the Houses of Parliament in 1842 and 1846 and later studied in Italy. His works include portraits of many famous contemporaries which he gave during his lifetime to the National Gallery, as well as historical and genre paintings. He was also a gifted sculptor.

WEBER, Max. American School. 1881. (Pages: 292, 293.)—Born Bialystok, Russia, he came to America ten years later to study first at the Pratt Institute and eventually abroad with Laurens and Matisse. Serious study of Chinese, Persian and European primitive art has influenced his style, which was revolutionary in the early days of America's artistic experiments. He has won many prizes and occupies a unique place in the art of his adopted country, a must on the purchase list of leading museums, a writer and a figure of international importance.

WILLUMSEN, Ferdinand. Danish School. 1863. (Page: 249.)—Born at Copenhagen (Denmark) where he studied to become an architect. Then he settled in Paris for several years, and traveled a great deal.

WHISTLER, James McNeill. American School. (Pages: 114, 133, 160, 161, 254.) Born in Massachusetts, his first art study was in St. Petersburg, Russia, where his father was engaged in an engineering project. After unsuccessful essays at a military career, he entered the studio of Gleyre in Paris. In 1859, he settled in England, achieving some success. Leading figure in a controversial case against Ruskin, he was known as an æsthete and wit. The portrait of the artist's mother, now in the Louvre, was acquired by the Luxembourg in 1891.

WILKIE, Sir David. Scottish School. 1785-1841. (Pages: 109,111.)—The son of a minister, he studied at Edinburg and London, and exhibited with great success in 1806 at the Royal Academy, where he was elected member in 1811. Three years later he visited Paris and in 1824 traveled in Italy and Spain; his style then changed and the charm of his genre paintings gave way to somewhat high-flown historical pictures. He received a great many distinctions and was knighted in 1836. In 1840 he visited the Middle East and on his return voyage he died and was buried at sea off Gibraltar, which inspired Turner's famous picture at the Tate Gallery.

WOOD, Christopher. English School. 1901-1930. (Pages: 270, 271, 272.)—Born at Knowsley near Liverpool. His father a doctor. A serious illness at the age of 14 interrupted his school studies for three years. 1921 went to Paris to study at Julian's. Traveled continuously in Europe in the ensuing years. 1926 worked in Paris designing a ballet for Diaghileff, which was never produced. 1927 first exhibition London. 1929 worked in Brittany and Cornwell. Died 1930.

WOOD, Grant. American School. 1892-1942. (Pages: 303, 306.)—Born in Iowa of Quaker stock, he began to draw the farm scenes he saw around him when still a boy, doing chores to help the family income. His art training was in Minneapolis and the Chicago Art Institute during the night hours, supported by daytime jobs. Later he settled in Cedar Rapids, Iowa, building his own house, teaching art in the public schools. Between 1920 and '28 he made four trips to Europe, doing some study at the Académie Julian, then returned to Iowa for good, founding the Stone City art colony which played an important part in the regional movement of the country. To-day his pictures are rarities of great value, the body of his work being in collections public and private.

WYANT, Alexander H. American School. 1836-1897. (Pages: 158, 166.) Born at Evans Creek, Ohio, he came under the influence of Inness. In 1864, a patron enabled him to go to New York to study, and later Germany and England. Though he traveled in the West, his favorite subject in landscape was the Catskills.

WYETH, Andrew. American School. 1917. (Page: 334.)—Born in Chadds Ford, Pennsylvania, the son of a well-known painter and illustrator, he held his first exhibition at the age of twenty, selling every item in the show. Regular one-man shows have followed, also a prominent place in the Museums of Modern Art's "Magic Realist" exhibit. In 1947 Wyeth received the Medal of Merit given by the American Academy of Arts and Letters and soon after won second prize at the Carnegie. Museums that own his work include the Metropolitan, Boston and the Art Institute of Chicago.

Z

ZULOAGA, Ignacio. Spanish School. 1870-1945. (Pages: 122, 123.) — Brought up in Paris from childhood, he worked without a master and later went to Rome. When not quite twenty, he returned and settled in Montmartre. Mallarmé, Gauguin, Degas and Rodin were his friends. He made a great impression at the Salon of 1914, but even before the end of the 19th century he was an acknowledged master of the Spanish national tradition. In 1901 he was elected to the Société Nationale des Beaux-Arts.

9841-11-50. — IMP. CRÉTÉ, CORBEIL

DÉPOT LÉGAL : 4e TRIMESTRE 1950.